THE BIG BOOK
OF MANAGEMENT

Tools and Techniques Every Manager Needs in Their Toolbox

THE BIG BOOK OF MANAGEMENT

Tools and Techniques Every Manager Needs in Their Toolbox

By

Komlan Joel Adzeh, PhD

With:
Joseph L. Almond, Catherine Farlow,
Desyra Highsmith, Brenda D. Kitchen, MBA,
SC Matheny, Malcolm O. Munro, Jeffrey Salters,
Tom Strickler, and Denise F. Williams

First Edition

Main Line Press . Montgomery Village, MD

©Main Line Press. All rights reserved (6/2013)

The Big Book of Management
Tools and Techniques Every Manager Needs in Their Toolbox

No part of this publication may be reproduced, stored in a retrieval system or transmitted in any form or by any means, electronic, mechanical, photocopying, recording, scanning or otherwise, except as permitted under code 107 or 108 of the 1976 United States Copyright Act, without the prior written permission of the Authors. Requests to the Author for permission should be addressed to Main Line Press, P.O. Box 2423, Montgomery Village MD 20886.

ISBN 978-0-9895795-0-6

Printed in the United States of America

Cover Layout
By
Michael Cartwright
mcartwright@comcast.net

*For
Our Families, Friends, Colleagues, Teachers,
Students, and Mentors*

*And all those who attend and participate in our
seminars and workshops!*

Table of Contents

Foreword

"Management"

It's been used as a noun and as a verb. Usually it's that group of people who come up with new and unpopular policies (*"Cell phone use is prohibited in this area...Management"*). It's parodied and scoffed at on television shows. Most of the time, managers are depicted as brown-nosing morons who mindlessly create and get caught up in bureaucracy.

We beg to disagree!

As a coalition of management and organizational development experts, we've spent our lives coaching and consulting with managers in all types and sizes of organizations. Our lessons learned and lessons taught are the focus of this book. We believe that management is a sacred role and, properly done, results in the greatest level of efficiency.

We believe managers are developed through a process of education, coaching, and progressively more challenging assignments. I use the model of the triangle because it reminds us of the Fire Triangle model used by firefighters. A fire is composed of three elements: heat, oxygen, and fuel. To put it out, just remove one element.

This works the same way in management development. The three elements are technical skill, quality of thinking, and interpersonal mastery. Remove one, and the whole thing collapses.

Here's how we define the elements:

Managerial Effectiveness: This is your ability to be a great manager. The manager's job is to make sure all functions are functioning and all people are performing to their maximum potential.

Technical Skills. These are the skills used to become an expert in a particular field. It could be anything from blue-collar trade skills to engineering. Technical skills normally don't mesh with supervision although you may have to work with people. There are some technical aspects to the job as well such as the appraisal forms and progressive disciplinary processes to follow.

Quality of Thinking. This is the ability to think strategically and critically. Like a chess player who must think three moves ahead, so must you change your way of thinking from transactional to strategic.

Interpersonal Mastery. This is your ability to work with and relate to others. It involves effective communication, patience, and understanding of yourself and others.

An organization can have only one true leader. Management helps the leader get the organization moving forward together.

Effective management is the only way to determine if a person has the potential to lead an organization.

Thus, the effective manager should:

1. Neither micromanage nor espouse a culture of benign neglect
2. Neither be a bully nor a spineless wimp
3. Maintain a culture of continuous learning

4. Seek out the root cause of every problem before attempting to solve it
5. Make employee performance management a high priority
6. Create and sustain a "full speed" work tempo
7. Refuse to accept poor performance. Deal with it swiftly and decisively
8. Recognize great performance
9. Constantly scout for talent, at all levels
10. Encourage innovation and creativity
11. Be an active delegator. Use delegation to grow yourself and your direct reports
12. Commit to their own continuous learning and development
13. Confront problems and conflicts
14. Accept, but not succumb to organizational politics
15. Use, but not abuse power
16. Advocate for what's right, even if it's unpopular
17. Build a working rapport with everyone
18. Always teach, coach, and mentor
19. Celebrate, but document, all success
20. Address, dissect, and find root causes of failures
21. Respect and leverage differences
22. Tie every action to "the big picture"
23. Stress the power of networking
24. Always reflect, always learn

Management skills are built through teaching, coaching, and mentoring. They are honed through reading and reflective journaling.

In this compilation of essays and strategies, you'll learn:

- How to make better decisions
- Strategies to develop a cohesive culture
- Ways to leverage different personalities
- Indicators of decreasing engagement

- Tools to leverage diversity and inclusion
- Management secrets of NFL coaching legends
- How to deal with difficult people
- Processes to increase employee engagement
- Easy ways to implement a LEAN culture
- Ways to avoid being (and how to deal with) toxic bosses

Who are the Authors?

This book is essentially a "Greatest Hits Collection" of some of the brightest and most experienced managerial experts I know.

Komlan Joel Adzeh, PhD.
An international scholar with expertise in organizational management.

Joseph L. Almond
A consultant with expertise in diversity and inclusion leadership and transformation.

Catherine Farlow
A burgeoning practitioner who takes complex organizational development topics and communicates them creatively.

Desyra Highsmith
A Human Resources expert who has grown a heightened sensitivity to the "human" element impacting learning, engagement and both individual and corporate growth.

Brenda D. Kitchen, MBA
A management consultant who specializes in facilitation, change management, organizational development and coaching.

SC Matheny
A former chaplain for the New York Jets NFL team who has observed and documented the techniques of successful (and unsuccessful) coaches.

Jeffrey Salters
An experienced consultant and trainer with expertise in building engaged work cultures in the public and private sector.

Tom Strickler
A technical management expert who has worked with many corporations and government agencies in developing innovative new processes to boost efficiencies.

Denise F. Williams
A retired Army Colonel with over 30 years of experience developing future leaders.

It's been an incredible experience connecting with these experts and having them combine their experience into a great resource for building management skills.

Management development is a journey. Use this book as your roadmap to get the most out of your people and develop the knowledge and skills to be an awesome boss!

Towards your Total Managerial Success,

Malcolm O. Munro
President, Total Career Mastery, LLC

Chapter 1

Eight-Step Model of Decision-Making: A Practical Guide for Managers and Leaders

By

Komlan Joel Adzeh, PhD.

The ability to make timely and effective decisions when confronted with uncertainty, complexity, and risks, has always been one of the important skills in organization management and a fine line between success and failure. Great responsibility comes with high expectations and it is not certain that good leaders will always make good decisions. Decision-making is the process of accurately assessing a problem and making the best use of the information and resources available to achieve the best possible outcome. Regardless of the nature of the organization, whether it is a non-profit, public, or private business, leaders have to decide the course of action to take in order to achieve their goals.

It is often assumed that in the organization, only the CEOs, senior executives, managers, and supervisors carry the responsibility of making a decision. As Peter Drucker pointed out, *"Most discussions of decision making assume that only senior executives make decisions or that only senior executives' decisions matter. This is a dangerous mistake."* The truth of the matter is that all management functions involve decision-making in one way or another. Whether your job is planning, organizing, staffing, directing, controlling[1], or any combination of these functions, at some point you need to make a decision regarding the most effective way to achieve your goal. Even our life is about making choices. You may not choose how, when or where you were born but you can choose where and how to live your life, what career to pursue, what to consume, etc. Albert Camus, a French novelist and winner for 1957 Literature Nobel Prize, once wrote, *"Life is the sum of all your choices."* The Greek philosopher Pythagoras (570 BC - 495 BC) argued, *"Choices are the hinges of destiny."* In other words, we live by making choices and the choices we make define our lives. Decision-making is the process of making the right choices.

In today's fast-paced competitive environment, effective, timely, and accurate decisions can be the difference between success and failure for businesses. Examples of decision-making success stories do not spread fast and they are quickly forgotten. However, the bad ones come to mind very easily. In the mid-1980s,

---

[1] Davey, H. W. (1956). Principles of management: An analysis of managerial functions Cornell University, School of Industrial & Labor Relations. *Industrial and Labor Relations Review 9*(2), 321-322

Coca-Cola Company made a decision to launch a new beverage product. The company was convinced that taste was the single most significant factor behind the decline of its market share. A new product was developed and was labeled New Coke, which was sweeter than the original formula. Nearly 200,000 tests were conducted in the United States and an overwhelming number of participants favored the taste of the New Coke over the original formula. However, did that mean consumers wanted to get rid of their old Coke? If the Coca-Cola Company had specifically asked the question, they would have known the answer. Instead, the Company launched the New Coke and withdrew the original formula from the market. That was the first change in the Coca-Cola formula in 99 years[23]. It turned out to be a bad decision and one of the biggest market research fiascos of all times. This decision cost the company millions of US dollars. Eventually, the company withdrew the new product and reintroduced the original formula into the market as Classic Coke. You should be asking yourself, what went wrong in the decision-making process, shouldn't you?

A more recent example that comes to mind is the story of the 2010 Toyota sticking gas pedal. Failure of Toyota

---

[2] Mikkelson, B.(May 19, 2011). "Knew Coke / New Coke Origin". Snopes.com. Retrieved May 04, 2013.
[3] Conversations Staffs (November 14, 2012)." The Real Story of New Coke". The Coca-Cola Company. Retrieved May 05, 2013.

Motor Corporation to make the tough decision to quickly acknowledge the unattended acceleration caused by the so-called sticking gas pedals resulted in 10 million vehicles being recalled worldwide, over 2 billion US dollars in expenses and sales lost, and a fine of 48.8 million US dollars. According to the industry guidelines, automakers are required to inform the U.S. National Highway Traffic Safety Administration within five days of discovering a defect in their vehicles[45]. Here again, what went wrong? Surely, whoever was responsible for making such an enormous decision was not fully prepared.

Another recent story of failed decision-making was the one that was broadcast in the news on April 08, 2013 with the replacement of JC Penny CEO, Ron Johnson with Mike Ullman[6]. Mr. Ullman was JC Penney's previous CEO and will most likely serve as an interim CEO until a new executive is found. In 2011, Johnson took over JC Penny and made the risky decision of trying to transform the "promotional department store" into a "specialty store." The company eliminated sales, coupons, and promotional discounts in favor of an everyday low price strategy.

[4] The U.S. Department of Transportation –DOT (2011). U.S. Department of Transportation
Releases Results from NHTSA-NASA *Study of Unintended Acceleration in Toyota Vehicles.* Retrieved May 05, 2013.

[5] US Recall News (2009*). Toyota Recalls 3.8 Million Vehicles: Gas Pedals Sticking.* Retrieved May 05, 2013

[6] Strauss. G, & Malcolm, H.(April 10, 2013) *Johnson out, ex-CEO Ullman in at J.C. Penney.* USA TODAY Retrieved May 05, 2013

During the 16-month experiment, the company's once loyal customers withdrew their business. Consequently, total revenue dropped 28.4 percent, JC Penny shares plunged more than 50 percent, and for the fiscal year, JC Penny lost $985 million. Despite a series of new initiatives that Johnson announced, including replacing older brands with new ones and even offering free haircuts for kids, he was not successful in revitalizing the company.

As a leader or a manager, no matter how important or insignificant your role is in the organization, eventually, you will be confronted with a situation where you will need to make a tough decision. It may not be of the same magnitude as the decision of Coca-Cola, Toyota, or JC Penny but it will be important to your organization nonetheless. The challenge is knowing how you can prepare yourself and be familiar with tools and techniques that can guide you to a successful outcome. If you ever find yourself in the position where your gut feeling is not enough to make a successful decision, this guide may be what you need. The purpose of this chapter is to propose what I have identified as the Eight-Step Model of Decision-Making. In the following pages, we will review together each one of these steps and summarize various tools and techniques that can be used to make effective decisions. Before doing so, however, we need to examine what people mean by decision-making.

Decision-Making Defined

There is a plethora of quotes relating to Decision-Making. Let us examine just a few.

- *"Whenever you see a successful business, someone once made a courageous decision."*
  –Peter F. Drucker

- *"Decision is a sharp knife that cuts clean and straight; indecision, a dull one that hacks and tears and leaves ragged edges behind it." –Gordon Graham*

- *"Man is man because he is free to operate within the framework of his destiny. He is free to deliberate, to make decisions, and to choose between alternatives." –Martin Luther King, Jr.*

- *"When it is not necessary to make a decision, it is necessary not to make a decision."*
  –Lord Falkland

- *"Good decisions come from experience. Experience comes from making bad decisions."*
  –Mark Twain

- *"Remember, a real decision is measured by the fact that you've taken new action. If there's no action, you haven't truly decided." –Tony Robbins*

- *"Again and again, the impossible problem is solved when we see that the problem is only a tough decision waiting to be made." –Robert H. Schuller*

- *"The quality of decision is like the well-timed swoop of a falcon which enables it to strike and destroy its victim." –Sun Tzu*

- *"Never bring the problem solving stage into the decision making stage. Otherwise, you surrender yourself to the problem rather than the solution." – Robert H. Schuller*

- *"When you make a decision, you need facts. If those facts are in your brain, they're at your fingertips. If they're all in Google somewhere, you may not make the right decision on the spur of the moment." –Ken Jennings*

- *"As soon as questions of will or decision or reason or choice of action arise, human science is at a loss." – Noam Chomsky*

- *"If you make the tough decisions, people will hate you today. But they will thank you for generations."* – The Iron Lady

- *"Once you make a decision, the universe conspires to make it happen."* –Ralph Waldo Emerson

- *"When you have to make a choice and don't make it, that is in itself a choice."* –William James

- *"Nothing is more difficult, and therefore more precious, than to be able to decide."* –Napoleon Bonaparte

As you can see, there is not a single definition of decision-making. People have thought about it and they have expressed various views and opinions about what it is and what it is not. However, the recurrent theme suggests that decision-making is important, difficult, and it can help achieve a successful outcome if the appropriate steps are taken. The more managers and organizations' leaders understand the decision making process the better they will be able to make good decisions, which brings me back to my initial goal of providing you with a systematic mechanism and tools that can help you make the right decision. Chances are, eventually you will have to decide what changes need to occur in your organization and what direction to take in order to remain relevant and competitive.

Mapping the Decision-Making Process

Now that we have explored what it means to make a decision, the challenges, and the implications that it involves, it is important to have a direction to follow when a situation arises. Most people in the organization are caught off guard when problems occur because they are not prepared. One of the basic principles of organization management is to continually assess the environment– both internal and external– and anticipate any future change. It is always good to have a strategy in place and be able to solve problems. However, anticipating those problems and making the tough decisions early in order to prevent them from occurring is a different skill set for effective leaders. When it comes to decision-making most people make the mistake of just talking about problem solving. Making a decision is far more complex than solving a problem. These are two different skill sets although they may overlap sometimes. Are you familiar with managers who often complain about their leaders being good at making decisions but they are nowhere to be found when it comes to solving problems or managers who are good at solving problems but who cannot take ownership of their decisions? Solving a problem is generally a temporary solution to an uncomfortable situation but a decision goes as far as turning a situation completely around or changing permanently the course of an event. Therefore, effective decision-makers seek to solve, not only an existing problem, but also to anticipate future unfavorable situations.

There are two models for making effective decisions: the rational and the irrational model. However, most management practitioners agree that problems facing organizations are too complex and the risks are too enormous to rely on the gut alone. In addition, framing the decision-making process can be a difficult task and a challenge for even a very talented leader. Some theories on decision-making have gone so far as to suggest that there is nothing rational about human behaviors. Of course, there are some ontological and epistemological differences in the way both positivists and interpretivists perceive reality. However, the premise of *Management* as a scientific discipline is based on the positivist worldview according to which, social facts are objective and measurable and therefore, they can be understood using a structured, rational, and logical approach. Such debate is beyond the scope of this chapter. Nonetheless, you are certainly familiar with Trevor Hastie, Robert Tibshirani, and Jerome Friedman's quote: *"In God we trust, all others bring data."* The proposed *Eight-Steps Model of Decision-*

Making outlines the steps that leaders and managers can follow to make a logical and rational decision. Under each step, we will review a number of tools and techniques that have been proven effective.

- Environment
- Problem
- Challenge
- Alternative

- Selection
- Communication
- Action
- Evaluation

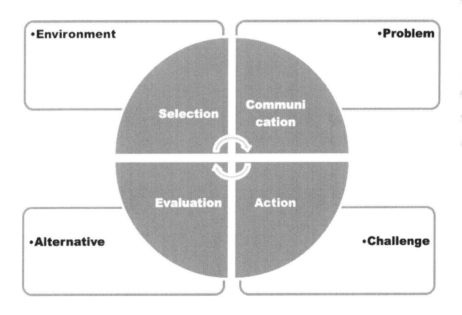

Eight-Step Model of Decision-Making

Eight-Step Model of Decision-Making

Step 1: Create a healthy internal organizational environment

Organizational environment influences the abilities of leaders and managers to make effective decisions. Various management studies suggest that employees, who are involved in their jobs, perceive organizational support, justice, fairness, and who trust their leaders, are likely to develop emotional attachments to their organizations' goals and values[7]. A healthy and constructive organizational environment fosters citizenship behavior, engagement, commitment, creativity, and willingness to take risk, which are important antecedents to successful decisions. Use the following techniques to involve the right people and build a cohesive team to tackle the problem. Make sure that you hear every one and everyone understands the way the final decision will be made.

- Use the *Stakeholder Analysis* to identify people who may have influence on the situation to be examined or the problem to be solved as well as the ones that may be impacted by the final decision.

---

[7] Adzeh, K. J. (2013). *Assessing the influence of organizational commitment on employee perceptions of superior customer value creation.* ProQuest, UMI Dissertations Publishing).

- Use the *Stepladder Technique* to select the right people and bring them gradually to the discussion table and make sure that they are all heard.
- Use the *Vroom and Yetton Model* to decide whether you will make the final decision on your own or you will need to have the consensus of your team, and then, adapt your leadership style.

Once you have identified the appropriate persons that should be involved in the process, established the objective, and clarified the way the final decision will be made, you can move on to the next step.

Step 2: Identify, define, and clarify the situation or the problem

Problem sensitivity is an important characteristic trait for effective leaders. However, decision-making requires more than being able to detect when something is going wrong or is likely to go wrong. At this stage in the process, you need to identify the specific situation or problem that you are trying to solve, define its scope, and clarify your understanding with the stakeholders. The following techniques can help making sure that you are solving the right problem and your decision will address the real issue facing your organization.

- Use the *Appreciative Inquiry* technique to build the decision-making process upon the strengths of the organization, rather than simply focusing on its weaknesses. This technique engages your team in a discussion about what the perfect solution might be and encourages innovative suggestions.

- Use the *5 Whys* to get to the root cause of the problem. Some practitioners suggest that by asking "why" five times, you will likely get to the root cause of the real problem and identify potential solutions.

- Use the *Reframing Matrix* to look at the problem from several perspectives.

- Use the *Affinity Diagrams* to identify relationships in the ideas you have gathered and structure them into small groups of similar information. The assumption here is that problems do not occur in isolation. This technique helps identify a pattern in the problem.

- Use the *Concept Fan* to redefine the problem if necessary. When the obvious solutions are not leading you in the right direction, this tool helps you to take "one step back" and broaden the scope of the problem.

Step 3: Evaluate the challenges

Organizations face problems that present different challenges. At this stage in the decision making process, you need to understand the level of uncertainty, complexity, and risks that the situation presents. Identify the unknowns, the interrelations between the components, and evaluate the way your final decision may affect your personal relationships.

- Use the *Brainstorming* technique to generate spontaneous ideas on possible challenges facing the organization. Do not criticize ideas that may sound crazy or reward the ones that you find exciting. The goal here is to encourage creative thinking.

- Use the *Six Thinking Hats* technique to invite the decision-making team members to wear the same hat at the same time so that they can focus their attention on one aspect of the challenge at a time.

- Use *Risk Analysis* to evaluate the threats and the likelihood that they materialize. This technique helps you understand the potential risks and mitigate their impact on the outcomes.

- Use the *Impact Analysis* technique to analyze the unexpected consequences that your decision may have on the organization. When things go wrong, we always wish that we had thought through the decision a little better. This is the time to ask yourself what could go wrong. By the time you have become aware of a problem, made a decision, and taken action, things might have changed.

Therefore, it is important to take into consideration the unintended consequences and how they could affect your organization.

Step 4: Synthesize, analyze, and evaluate plausible alternatives

At this step in the decision-making process, you might have already come up with several alternative solutions to the problem you are facing. Now is the time to begin narrowing down the potential solutions. Most importantly, avoid *Groupthink*. The solution that the majority of the team members approve may not necessarily be the right one.

- Use *Cost-Benefit Analysis* to add up the total benefits of a particular approach to the problem and compare it with the total costs.
- Use *Paired Comparison Analysis* to make sure you are not comparing apples to oranges when you are evaluating different alternatives.
- Use *Grid Analysis* to make sure that you take into consideration various factors that, when put together, may contribute to the best possible solution.
- Use *Prioritization* to classify the alternative solutions according to the time constraint and available resources.

- Use *Pareto Analysis* aka *"80/20 Rule"* to decide which problems you can solve by just making some changes in the organization's operations so that you can focus your full attention on the most difficult issues.

Step 5: Select the best alternative

Experienced decision-makers may be tempted to get to the final decision right away by trusting their gut. However, the tools and techniques that are suggested here will lead you to making a more rational and systematic decision. At this stage, the task is to select the best possible solution, not necessarily the one that will make everyone happy, but the one that has the best probability of being successful.

- Use the *Nominal Group Technique* to rank all the alternative solutions and select the one with the highest ranking, particularly when the final decision has to be made as a team.
- Use *SWOT analysis* to identify the strengths, weaknesses, opportunities, and threats that each alternative presents.
- Use the *Satisficing* technique to select the solution that meets the minimum requirements rather than trying to achieve optimization, particularly when other solutions come with higher cost and risk.

- *Cost and Benefit Analysis* can also be helpful in selecting the best possible solution.
- Use the *Analytic Hierarchy Process (AHP)* to weigh various subjective factors that can have a significant impact on the final decision. Not all decision criteria are straightforward. Some may include intangible and subjective factors based on individual preferences or priorities. This tool combines both quantitative and qualitative aspects of all the decision criteria into a standardized scale that can help assign a numerical weight to each possible solution and make a rational decision.
- Most importantly, use the *Ladder of Inference* technique to avoid jumping to a quick conclusion. At this point, you may be leaning toward the "best" solution, but take a moment to check your preferences against your own biases and assumptions, and make sure that you remain objective throughout the process.
- Finally, conduct a *Blind Spot Analysis* to ascertain the quality of the final decision over other alternatives.

Step 6: Communicate your decision

Decision communication can be a challenging task. A single *faux pas* at this stage can compromise the effort that has been put in the process so far. Therefore, this step should be planned carefully. Decision-makers should address each aspect of this step by deciding who should communicate the final decision, what to include in the message, which channel of communication to use, and how to monitor employee response. The following process is designed to help you improve your decision communication skills.

- Identify the right person to communicate the final decision in order to gain immediate attention and credibility. Generally, this person should be a high-ranking member of the organization, an icon, the CEO.
- Design the message carefully by linking it to the core values, the mission statement, and the goal of the organization.
- Highlight the key steps that have led to the final decision in order to build trust.
- Emphasize that you understand the impact that the decision may have on the employees and your willingness to address individual concerns.
- Use both oral and written channels to deliver the message in order to get as much attention as possible.
- Put in place an *open door* policy to address misunderstanding, misconception, or misrepresentation. Experience has shown that

employees will embrace your decision, endure it, or passively reject it. Either way, you need to monitor the reactions and make sure you get your point across without being insensitive to their concerns.

Step 7: Take action

A decision must be followed with an action plan in order for organizations to achieve their expected results, otherwise, it would remain only a good intention. Managers involved in the implementation of the decision should identify and allocate the resources needed to achieve the organizational goals. Five methods contribute to a successful implementation of decisions and they all relate to the primary functions of management, as indicated by Harold Koontz and Cyril O'Donnell:

– *Planning:* This is not the time to be asking the reason why a decision has been made. Rather, focus on what to do, when, and how to do it. Action planning is more than a To-Do-List. Be as specific as possible by including every single detail and timelines. Think about tasks that you can accomplish by yourself and the ones that you will delegate. Tools such as Gantt Charts, PERT Charts, and Critical Path Analysis can come in handy in sorting through your priorities, allocating the resources, and identifying the best way to meet deadlines.

- *Organizing:* Divide the workload into subgroups, organize your team, and assign responsibilities by making sure that the right people are in charge of the right tasks.
- *Staffing:* This step needs to be planned ahead of time through ongoing training and development programs. However, in cases of urgency, you may need to solicit specialized staffing agencies to bring on board the specific skills that you need to achieve your goals.
- *Leading:* Guide, direct, motivate, and support your team. Demonstrate self-discipline and commitment to the goal. You may need to adjust your leadership style to the circumstance; and more important, lead by example.
- *Controlling:* Although the word "control" may lead to misinterpretation, it is immensely helpful to have a mechanism in place to anticipate, identify, measure, and rectify any deviation from organizational standards and policies. Tools such as Return on Investment (ROI), Benchmarking, Budget Variance Analysis, Project Cycle Time, Customer Satisfaction Index, Employee Satisfaction Survey etc. can help measure the progress the organization is making toward achieving its objective.

Throughout the decision implementation phase, effective decision-makers should understand that things might go wrong between the decision and the implementation time. Therefore, it is recommended to perform *What If Analysis* in order to analyze how change in the initial condition that led to the decision could affect the successful implementation of the actions that are being taken. Also, be willing to adjust the action plan whenever it is necessary.

Step 8: Evaluate your decision

When it is all said and done, a good decision-maker will look back and ask whether the initial objective has been achieved and whether there is anything, he or she could have done differently. Decision evaluation involves learning from a mistake and preparing for the future. There are two methods of decision evaluation, formative evaluation and summative evaluation. While formative evaluation is used throughout the implementation phase to identify dysfunctions and to make changes, the summative evaluation is conducted ex-post in order to collect information on the extent to which the intended goal has been achieved. Tools such as surveys, questionnaires, interviews, or focus groups can be very helpful in identifying what went wrong and at what moment exactly in the process. For impartial analysis, it is recommended that someone outside the organization conduct this type of evaluation.

Getting a competitive edge in a post-recession economy requires making tough and smart decisions. The purpose of the *Eight-Step Model of Decision-Making* is to simplify the rational decision-making model in a meaningful way and to provide organizations' leaders and managers with a structured process including tools and techniques that have been proven effective in the management practice. Effective leaders understand the challenges that are involved and what it takes to make changes in order to remain competitive. While there is no infallible model of decision-making, it is commonly accepted that a rational approach, as described in this chapter, is likely to minimize decision failure. By embracing a systematic and logical approach to making important decisions, leaders and managers can be confident that they are writing the next chapter in the success story of their organizations.

About Komlan Joel Adzeh, PhD:

Dr. Adzeh is an Associate Consultant at Total Career Mastery, LLC and a leading scholar-practitioner who has brought a new insight into the discipline of organization management. He holds a Master of Science in Business Management, an MBA in Acquisition, and a Doctorate degree in Organization and Management.

Chapter 2

Thermostat or Thermometer?

By

Joseph L. Almond

For as long as I can remember I have asked managers if they were a thermometer or a thermostat. When asked there is usually an uncomfortable silence that occurs. I then ask them "What is the function of a thermometer?" Someone will inevitably raise their hand in order to respond. Without fail they say the function of a thermometer is to gauge the temperature. I say how many managers do you know that can give you the temperature of the work environment? They can tell you if things are going well or not, what the climate is without regulating it. It seems they think by assessing the climate of the work environment they are actually having an impact. I then ask what the function of a thermostat is. Again someone will raise their hand and reply a thermostat regulates the climate. I then ask which manager are you? Of course there is once again an awkward silence.

Managers set the climate for their organizations. Managers have the responsibility to regulate the climate for their leadership as well as for their employees. This is a responsibility that can sometimes be taken lightly. Based upon experiences I have had as a consultant, employees hold their managers to a standard of excellence. The managers who understand that employees are investing a portion of their lives in the workplace are seeking to create a great work experience for their employees. They understand employees have an expectation of their organization and management. Therefore employees are looking for the best ROI possible. Employees are trading their time for money. It has become very important for employees to work in environments where they feel a sense of comfort. Managers who understand their influence on the work environment provide the leadership needed to regulate the climate in order to meet or even exceed employee expectations.

Many people know what it's like to work in an environment that has challenged every fiber of their being. Perhaps the challenge is the job itself, another employee, or even the manager. The stress can be much greater when there is manager who is not regulating the climate in a way that supports all of their employees. The days of do as I say not as I do are long gone. If you have ever seen the Missouri license plate you know that their tag line is 'The show me state." Mangers need to make that line a reality in the environments. Employees are not looking for their managers to bury heads in the sand, be passive aggressive or MIA in the workplace. They are looking for managers who hold themselves and others to the highest standards possible to get their jobs done with excellence as the benchmark.

I have had the pleasure of working with managers in numerous organizations around the world. There are many reasons why some managers have had successes while others haven't even though they were in the same organization with the same resources to draw from. One reason for success I have consistently noticed is whether the manager was proactive by setting and regulating the climate or merely being reactive by gauging only. Gauging the climate of the environment is necessary however that is just a part of the expectation of a great manager. Once the temperature has been gauged it's very important for the manager to make adjustment to the climate as necessary. This is where managers who are thermostats distinguish themselves from the managers who are thermometers.

I joined the United States Army at the age of seventeen. When I look at leadership and management styles I have a lot of examples to choose from. Often people assume that the military is all about giving and receiving orders. Sometimes there is a one size fits all philosophy thought to be prevalent in the military. This is not always the case. Even though orders are giving to ensure the integrity of the mission is not compromised. There are some amazing examples of how soldiers in the civilian world some would be called "managers" have set the tone in the most difficult of circumstances. I started my leadership experience as a nineteen year old with responsibility for several other soldiers. I learned early in my military service that there were numerous things outside my control and above my pay grade. However the one thing I had control over always was my attitude.

Attitude is probably one of the most talked about subjects however still one of the most powerful things to manage. In order for a manager to regulate the climate of their environment they must know to self-manage and self-regulate their attitudes. Years ago I was supporting a mission in the Mojave Desert. My troops and I had been there for weeks and tension was high based on the less than cool temperatures and the stressful work conditions. Some of the soldiers were getting frustrated and were looking forward to going home. Honestly as was, however that was not going to happen any time soon. I made a conscious decision with a couple others to "Be" the example and regulate the climate. We couldn't do a thing about the physical climate of a hundred plus degrees daily. We did have control over our personal thermostat which radiated and consumed those around us to make the climate adjustment that would prove to be valuable to all. I think too many time managers are feeling as though they don't have the power to change things at their level. Managers must assume the responsibility of being the thermostat in their work for their employees. However it must start with regulating themselves.

Managers must be willing to get out of their personal comfort zones when it comes to looking at the manager in the mirror. You have heard so many times before we must ask ourselves are we part of the problem or part of the solution. Once we can honestly answer that question we can begin to make a shift in our attitudes in order to impact those whom we work with. To regulate or not to regulate...that is the question. It will take and honest assessment of ourselves that many will choose not to make. Many managers are comfortable managing process, executing the strategies that leadership has created, and maintaining the status quo. Great managers understand their attitude impacts their altitude and this has a tremendous influence on the employees alike. Remember employees are listening less to what we say but watching everything we do or don't do.

When I served as a Vice President of Training years ago I found out just how important it was for me to make attitude adjustments along the way. I had ten to twelve consultants reporting to me at the time. We were working on a multi-year multimillion dollar project. My role was to select, train, schedule and monitor for quality assurance for the project. I had consultants that worked and lived across the United States. The team was filled with diversity in every dimension possible. It was important to the clients that no matter what the differences were we delivered quality service every time. I knew our collective attitude regulated the climate and it was one thing that united us a team. We were strong as a result of our differences versus being weak in spite of them. I learned to leverage the differences through setting the tone or the temperature for team environment. This would have been very difficult if the team had not bought into being the thermostats for the client. The attitude became very contagious within the team and with the client.

I noticed how when my attitude was positive and upbeat it had great pay value for us all. I also realized that if I were having a moment of frustration and negativity that would impact them equally as well. I learned to regulate the work environment with my team who didn't share a common work space however we shared common goal. This experience was an opportunity for me to stretch and get out of my comfort zone in order to grow. Change is inevitable...growth is optional. Change will happen with or without our consent. However we can choose to grow or not grow. Managers who are regulating their work environments are also liberating their work environments. Employees produce greater results in the long term when they feel valued and they can trust their management. Managers are setting a climate that employees can thrive in when they positively regulate the work environment. Employees will be a mirror image of their managers, the good, the bad, and the ugly.

Therefore as a manager I get to check myself and ask what temperature am I setting in my work environment? What am I creating in my space from day to day? Do I need to turn up the heat or cool things down a little? How are my employees experiencing me? Are they looking forward to seeing me come or to seeing me go? If the climate isn't where it needs to be what am I going to do about it. Many managers understand their responsibility roles to the organization. They can follow them to the letter. However when it comes to their accountability roles they fall short. Managers must feel a sense of accountability to their employees versus only feeling responsible for them. I worked with organizations that drive cultural change from top to bottom however not all understand how to empower their managers to create the climate that will drive the emergence of change agents.

These managers who are change agents regulate the climate to meet organizational goals. I worked with an organization a few years ago. This organization was a leader in their industry. They decided they wanted to be proactive and improve upon the organizational culture.

They hired outside consultants which is a very common practice. The manager that was spearheading the initiative was very committed to the success of the cultural change. He spent a great deal of his time looking at ways to improve upon his management style. He sought out books to read and workshops to attend. He knew in order for him to be the change agent he needed to be, he first needed to make some changes himself. He decided to get out of his comfort zone and take an honest assessment of where he was versus where he wanted to be. His team began to see his transformation. Within a year of the initiative rolling out he was not only able to get his team on board but also the leadership by setting the tone through his actions within the organization. He was now working with a team of change agents because they were able to acclimate to the climate he set for change. It all started within him. It then spread in his work environment within the team who then regulated the climate for others. The organization was recognized as leader throughout their industry for setting the climate for other organizations to follow. The manager set the tone first for himself, his team, and others in the industry.

This manager understood that in order for the initiative to truly have an impact he needed to allow the message of the initiative to impact him first. You can't sell what you don't believe. I've heard sales are nothing more than the transference of belief. If he had attempted to change the organizational culture on his own it would have been impossible. However when he worked on himself and when others saw the climate shift they shifted with it. The power of one manager's choice can impact many. Most of us have experienced a manager that is creating an environment where people grow and are thriving. We have also seen the manager that is creating an environment where people are dying or merely existing.

Managers have tremendous influence in work their environments. Managers must manage to get out of their own way and regulate the climate in their environments. What I have found that if managers are not regulating the climate someone else in the environment will. Sometimes that employee is stepping into the role of a thermostat out of necessity when the manager is MIA. This can be a good thing or it can lead to chaos and disaster depending on the employee's motivation. In essence someone is always regulating the climate. Are you a thermometer or a thermostat? The choice is yours.

About Joseph L. Almond:

Joseph Almond is an Army veteran, author, speaker and coach. He holds a Masters of Arts Degree in Organizational Leadership. He provides customized keynotes, coaching and training programs. His expertise in diversity and inclusion leadership and transformation has assisted numerous organizations.

Joseph brings his experience with government, schools, non-profit, and business to his presentations. He captures imaginations while stimulating the intellect. Since professional life is an extension of a person's personal life he incorporates relevant life experiences in a compelling way to connect deeply with his audiences.

He has over 20 years of professional speaking experience. He is the author of the book ***Get Better Not Bitter*** in which he inspires others to live their best life in the midst of adversity.

Joseph's diverse career has equipped him to interface with a multitude of individuals employed in a number of progressive organizations nationally and internationally. His expertise in leadership, diversity and military transition has assisted numerous organizations. His expertise in leadership, diversity and military transition has assisted numerous organizations.

Chapter 3

The "Fruits" of Personality

An Interpretation of Myers-Briggs Personality Types

By

Catherine Farlow

You can't compare apples and oranges. We've all heard this expression, but you can compare them. You just can't have the same expectations for apples and oranges; they are completely different in essence, texture, and taste. In the same way, some people are apples and some people are oranges. Their difference emanates from the core-- the seed of who they are as people.

Human personality is like a fruit seed. The seed is nurtured uniquely through one's upbringing, environment, and circumstances. Myers-Briggs typology is one interpretation of human personality, and it indicates that personality is inborn (the seed) and that one has an innate preference for one dichotomy over the other. Myers-Briggs typology is a tool that is helpful in team building, leadership and personal development as well as management. It examines four elements or dichotomies of personality- how one gains their energy, how one takes in information, how one makes decisions, and how one conducts their lifestyle.

Sun: One's Energy Flow Outwards or Inwards

The first element of personality, **extraversion (E)** or **introversion (I)** can be thought of as the sun—the direction of one's energy that is required to experience and sustain personal growth.

With **extraversion**, the sun beams outwardly. Not only is one fed by external interaction, but their energy is directed outward to merge with their experiences at hand. Extraverts are fed by contact with other people and through participating in activity. They soak up energy from engaging with the world and people around them. Extraverts' attention is magnetized to people, objects, and activity. Verbal processing or speaking to think tends to be the dominant mode for the extravert. For the extravert, action and speech more often than not precede contemplation or reflection.

Confident extraverts may excel at "thinking on their feet" because their natural mode of processing happens in the moment. Extraverts generally find talking to come more easily than intent listening. Extraverts may feel isolated and lethargic when they have been alone for stretches of time. In this case, they may seek out interaction, even with new people or strangers whereas an introvert would like hold back from initiating contact.

American culture promotes extraversion through an emphasis on group work, self-promotion, assertiveness ("the squeaky wheel gets the grease") and outgoing leadership.

With **introversion**, the sun beams inward. One's energy is directed inwards in an attempt to align the outer world and the inner world, and in the process, stimuli from the outer world is shut off to accomplish this integration. Introverts are fueled by retreating from activity and social interaction into the world of ideas and thoughts. Introverts attention is drawn to the world of ideas, and their intake of information is conceptualized subjectively. Their intake of information is selective, meaning that what is absorbed will likely be thoroughly sorted through and remembered. Solitude brings comfort and refreshment to the introvert. Introverts enjoy focusing deeply and also cultivating depth in a few select relationships. Introverts may frequently rehearse their words before speaking and may often walk away from a conversation or interaction wishing they had thought to say something else. Introverts quickly grow weary of repeating themselves and may not readily share their thoughts or opinions unless solicited.

Soil: How One Takes in Information

The second element of personality, **sensing (S)** or **intuition (N)**, can be thought of as the soil in which one is planted. Soil directly impacts the root system of the plant and its nutrient intake, and in the same way sensing and intuition serve as two distinctive types of soil producing a different intake of information.

People who prefer **sensing** are planted in the here and now. They are grounded, and they are aware of their environments. They gather information primarily through the five senses—seeing, hearing, touching, smelling, and tasting. They have a thorough grasp of the real world and reality. Sensors study "the trees" and appreciate concreteness. Sensors speak the language of specifics and prefer rules to undertones. They seek to communicate clearly, portraying their thoughts in a straightforward manner. Sensors tend to dislike theoretical or abstract matters, gravitating more to practical and predetermined facts. Past experiences help inform sensors current decisions.

People who prefer **intuition** look beyond where they are planted, thinking of possibilities and pressing into the future. They thrive by making connections and perceive of the world through what could be described of as a sixth sense. Intuitives are drawn towards imagining what the world could be versus the present reality of the world. Patterns and theories are an intricate part of their thought process. Vision and inspiration propel them, and they have a big picture or "forest" perspective. Pushing for innovation and liberation from routine, intuitives seek to pioneer new frontiers. For the most part, intuitives communicate in more metaphorical and roundabout ways than sensors.

Roots: How One Makes Decisions

The third element of personality, **thinking (T)** or **feeling (F)**, can be thought of as one's actual roots system. Roots gather nutrients and cultivate them to help produce the blossom. Thus, roots, although hidden from view much like one's internal thought processing and decision making, greatly impact the overall outcome of the fruit or in this case one's visible personality.

People who prefer **thinking** are rooted with logic. Thinkers base their decisions on data, and they detach themselves emotionally from others when making tough decisions. They are more task oriented than relational, and they enjoy finding solutions to problems. Thinkers may be harder to get to know than feelers. Their opinions tend to be deeply entrenched and based on impartial data. They consider the pros and cons of situations, and for the thinker to operate healthfully and comfortably, things must make sense to them. Thinkers appreciate conflict that brings clarity, and they place a higher value on justice than mercy.

People who prefer **feeling** are rooted with subjective values. Before they make a decision, feelers consider the impact of it on others. Feelers seek to please others, and they are generally interested in preserving harmony, even at a cost to themselves. Their decisions must feel right to them personally. Feelers channel their energies toward empathy and relationship. They communicate in a personable fashion, monitoring not only their own feelings but others. They win allegiance by personal appeals.

Fruit Blossom: One's Visible Lifestyle

The fourth element of personality, **judging (J)** or **perceiving (P)**, can be thought of as the blossom of a fruit plant-- the most outward signifier of personality.

People who prefer **judging** flourish when they are able to order their lives, accomplish goals, make expedient decisions, and bring about closure. Judgers prefer structure, especially if they have some control over it. Judgers are most comfortable when they have made a decision, and they have an internal clock that is always ticking. They have an awareness of dates and deadlines. Judgers live life by the motto of "work now, play later". When judgers communicate, they often let the other person know what role they expected to play whereas a perceiver may leave everything open-ended.

People who prefer **perceiving** blossom when serendipitous events are allowed to occur in their life because they are not committed to a strict schedule. Perceivers enjoy gathering information more than making decisions and they often put off making decisions until it has either been decided by default or they have reached reasonable clarity. Perceivers explore and are more interested in discovery than accomplishing tasks. Perceivers relish the power of the present moment and spontaneous freedom. Too much structure and regimentation cause the perceiver to grow restless. Perceivers often have difficulty staying on task, but they are generally more flexible than judgers.

The Fruits

There are 16 different personality types according to Myers-Briggs typology. These types are configured by one preference for each category discussed. In this chapter, a fruit has been chosen to symbolically represent each of the types.

ESTJ: "The Orange"
(Extravert-Sensing-Thinking-Judging)

Oranges are orderly. They are structured in a clear fashion with different sections, and likewise ESTJs are ordered and systematic. ESTJs are highly decisive, productive, and hard working individuals who like to be in charge. They are organizationally gifted, and they lead people to accomplish tangible goals. They have a regulated approach to life and are goal-oriented. They are objective and quintessential supervisors. They are in charge of themselves and are generally assertive people who cannot stand quitters. As managers, they ensure standards are met, goals are accomplished, and that appropriate positive and negative consequences are delivered. In communication with ESTJs, be objective and get to the point.

ISTJ: "The Grapefruit"
(Introvert-Sensing-Thinking-Judging)

Grapefruits are characterized by their internal organization, thick skin and not exactly sweet taste. All of these attributes could be applied to the ISTJ. ISTJs are painstakingly thorough and meticulous in what they do (internal organization) and they take things seriously. They have an innate awareness of what worked for them in the past and they are drawn to unchanging truths.

ISTJs are hard to get to know, and although they are quiet, they possess an iron will (thick skin). ISTJs are focused on tasks rather than people (not the sweetest fruit), but they are loyal and reliable despite their detachment. They are cautious by nature and are comfortable spending copious amount of time alone, immersed in projects or thoughts. They demonstrate an uncommon single-mindedness or an intense ability to focus on one thing and they prefer working alone. As managers, they assume their perspective is the correct way of thinking and they expect others to honor their commitments. ISTJs are careful managers of details. Their thoroughness is a great asset in the right position.

ESFJ: "The Banana"
(Extravert-Sensing-Feeling-Judging)

Bananas are wholesome and grow in clusters. The banana represents the ESFJ because of its friendly yellow color--ESFJs are often personable individuals who wear their emotions on their sleeves, not able to hide their "true colors". The banana's shape could symbolize the straight and narrow path, and the ESFJ typically acts with great conviction and has a clearly ingrained sense of what "should be" and what "should not be". ESFJs are deliberate yet compassionate, and they enjoy managing others. ESFJs have a need to control their environment, and they like to get things moving. They are expressive, orderly, and thorough. As managers, they sometimes let their emotions cloud their decision making but otherwise they are consistent and desire harmony. Oftentimes, ESFJs resist change. To win them over, use a people-centered approach and show them appreciation.

ISFJ: "The Blueberry"
(Introvert-Sensing-Feeling-Judging)

Blueberries are the oldest known fruit, and they are true blue; these characteristics make the blueberry a good metaphor for the ISFJ. ISFJs are the most loyal type—a true blue individual and friend. When everyone else flakes, the ISFJ is loyal to the end. They are caretaking individuals who show great devotion to even the least of these. They are meticulous with their work and follow rules. They pay attention to people's needs and seek to satisfy them. They are responsible, patient, and protective individuals who often work best behind the scenes. As a manager, the ISFJ is relational and specific. One of the keys to working with an ISFJ is not to rush them because they do their best work when they are allowed to be methodical and contemplative.

ENTJ: "The Pineapple"
(Extravert-Intuition-Thinking-Judging)

Pineapples contain an enzyme that is helpful in breaking down protein and they are distinctive ("large and in charge" you could say). ENTJs are powerful problem solvers who are able to break things down and grasp them quickly much like an enzyme at work. They bring order in chaos and they mobilize others. They call out competence in people, and they are self-confident individuals who are constantly self-improving. They are extremely action-oriented and they focus on long-term projections rather than details. When dealing with an ENTJ, state your point first and then break it down if necessary. They be tough (think pineapple skin). ENTJs view everything as an opportunity for leadership and they manage others directly. They enjoy new challenges and are global thinkers who can create and implement incredible strategies.

INTJ: "Grape Cluster"
(Introvert-Intuition-Feeling-Judging

Grape clusters are self-contained units with complex configurations. A grape cluster visually represents the self-sufficiency and independence of the INTJ, but yet at the same time the intricacy of the INTJ's thought-processing that connects disparate thoughts into one multifaceted whole. INTJs have great intellectual acumen, and they are driven towards self-improvement and intellectual challenges. Competency is their language, and they value knowledge. Their integrative thought process includes creative visions for the future that have never been conceived of before by others, and they have an internal vision of how to get from the present reality to this uncharted territory. They are the most independent type and are at their very essence masterminds. INTJs are constantly seeking to improve things and thus they do not offer much praise and when they do it is most certainly not in excess. They are long-range planners who are highly conceptual and task-focused, expecting competence from others.

ENTP: "The Lime"
(Extravert-Intuition-Thinking-Perceiving)

ENTPs are zesty like limes. They have charm, energy, and charisma. In the spotlight, they are ignited. They are resourceful, always squeezing the last drop out of what they can get. They are skilled communicators who are quick to point out their insights. They could be described as masters of adaptability who overcome challenges and gain energy from the process. They like to be liked and accent others well (like a lime accents many dishes). ENTPs see patterns and are talented in finding ingenious solutions to technical as well as interpersonal problems. They are very much focused on the big picture so too many details can burn them out, but they may need help prioritizing their work. As managers, ENTPs strive to help others clarify their own thinking and move into action. They are risk-takers who encourage independence and enterprising in others. If managing an ENTP, give them a creative challenge and they will likely design an efficient system.

INTP: "The Pomegranate"
(Introvert-Intuition-Thinking-Perceiving)

On the inside, pomegranates are elaborate, and much like this, the INTP is cognitively complex. The pomegranate self-pollinates, and the INTP derives much of their needed stimuli by devoting time to the life of their mind. INTPs are constantly striving to become experts, and their thoughts go through a constant refining process. INTPs ask hard questions and are quick to find inconsistencies. INTPs have intense focus and work long stretches well alone. They are ingenious, autonomous, and powerfully curious people. They are perfectionists who are mentally quick and independent problem solvers. To gain the INTP's respect, one must prove himself worthy. INTPs are gifted at designing and bringing coherence to systems, especially within the computer world.

ESTP: "The Watermelon"
(Extravert-Sensing-Thinking-Perceiving)

Watermelons are juicy and cheerful, and if you were to personify them, you could say they were full of life. ESTPs like watermelons add lightness to situations (or meals in the case of the fruit). ESTPs are unpredictable because they have a chameleon like ability to adapt. They learn from doing, are quick thinking, and make calculated risks. They know how to make the most of the moment and also how to influence people's perceptions of them. They love life and often are of good humor. ENTPs are versatile and straightforward. They like being where the action is and are assertive communicators. They are persuasive and have a winning persona that draws others towards them. They are observant and are pragmatic troubleshooters who can improvise easily. When managing an ESTP, provide stability and let them know what you need from them in a simple and clear manner.

ISTP: "The Cantaloupe"
(Introvert-Sensing-Thinking-Perceiving)

Cantaloupes have netted skin. ISTPs are careful observers, catching details others think they might miss because of their often detached demeanor. ISTPs are very independent and much of their thinking is hidden from view like the seeds inside of a cantaloupe. ISTPs are action driven problem solvers who prefer to raise questions rather than share their own thoughts. ISTPs feel little need to influence others, and thus they are not natural managers except from a distance. They resist regimentation, and their leadership style naturally is almost entirely leading through action rather than communication or brainstorming. ISTPs maintain composure in crisis situations and are able to calmly approach the issue. They have unmatched troubleshooting skills.

ESFP: "The Strawberry"
(Extravert-Sensing-Feeling-Perceiving)

Strawberries are widely liked for their sweetness, and their bright color is attractive. ESFPs are popular like strawberries. They lighten up any setting and they add an extra splash of color to life. They offer warmth and celebration of life. They accept people and are open and fun-loving. They can often be found in the spotlight due to their joyful living, outgoing demeanor, optimistic perspective, and desire to impact others. They are persuasive and observant. Managers may have a hard time pinning the ESFP down, but the ESFP can create excitement and enthusiasm unlike any other type.

ISFP: "The Peach"
(Introvert-Sensing-Feeling-Perceiving)

That's just peachy. ISFPs have this incredible knack for doing and saying the right thing at the right moment, and they put others at ease. They are unassuming and are very interested in serving others. ISFPs have a gentle nature but a strong internal core of values much like a peach has a soft exterior but a core that is hard to penetrate. ISFPs are harmonious and caring individuals, and they often are artistically gifted and extremely aware of their environment. They feel things through their senses. They are resourceful, and when managing them, it is helpful to appeal to their values and allow them space to think, if you want to maximize their creative potential. They are both cooperative and independent. One thing to never ask an ISFP to do is self-promote, this is against their modest nature. ISFPs communicate through actions rather than verbal expression so before offering correction if they are not contributing vocally to projects or meetings, examine their work.

ENFP: "The Mango"
(Extravert-Intuition-Feeling-Perceiving)

Mangos have an interesting exterior; the skin often showcasing a combination of several colors, and the interior flesh is bright with a pit in the middle. ENFPs are like mangos. Their outward appearance is contagious, and their inner depth is dynamic and bold. They also have an inner core of values. ENFPs are expressive and enthusiastic. They are curious and passionate and wild at heart. They are catalysts for change and charismatic leaders. People may begin to follow the ENFP without the ENFP stepping up for a position of leadership because they motivate others so naturally. The ENFP inspires others to reach their fullest potential, and one of the ways in which they do this is through generating numerous ideas and possibilities. ENFPs are project-oriented workers who particularly enjoy throwing themselves into something new. To manage an ENFP well, don't micro manage them but make sure they are saving some steam to follow the project to completion. ENFPs are consumed with the big picture, and they champion causes that match their internal core. They inspire leadership in others.

INFP: "The Nectarine"
(Introvert-Intuition-Feeling-Perceiving)

Nectarines are peaches without the fuzz. INFPs are similar to ISFPs (the peach) in many ways, but they gather information heavily through intuition. INFPs often occupy peacekeeper roles. They are intent listeners who value people's personal space. They work well alone without much supervision. They are free thinking and have deep passion for the causes they believe in. They have high standards for themselves and may exhibit intense concentration on personally meaningful projects. They orchestrate unity and harmony. There is more to the INFP than meets the eye. They are reserved but have a deep well of caring and passion. They work behind the scenes well and value relationships. They are curious and seek out information. They are deep people who may struggle to vocalize their thoughts, preferring to listen. As managers, INFPs are incredibly idealistic and everything is a reflection of their personal vision. They are not often in managerial positions but when they are, they may rely on a collaborative approach.

ENFJ: "The Plum"
(Extravert-Intuition-Feeling-Judging)

Plums are versatile fruits that can be eaten as is, dried, juiced, made into jam, and syrup. Plums are known for flushing the system, and although this comparison does not exactly sound flattering, ENFJs are healing people like plums. ENFJs help instill confidence in others and also help them fulfill their potential. ENFJs are adept at understanding people, and they are capable communicators. They are mentors and people oriented in their inner core. They lead with warmth and communication and they also facilitate and promote others in leadership. ENFJs are supportive leaders and much of their self-identity closely relates to their personal relationships. Because the ENFJ is always giving out, they need to receive as well. When ENFJs are not appreciated, they with and dry up like prunes. Managers should provide positive feedback to the ENFJ whenever the situation merits it; this affirmation will sustain the ENFJ who contributes in more ways than are probably readily apparent.

INFJ: "The Kiwi"
(Introvert-Intuition-Feeling-Judging)

From a kiwi's skin, you would never expect the complex pattern inside the fruit or the sweet unique flavor. INFJs are unique like kiwis. They are complex and reserved, you would not know from their appearance how inwardly warm and sensitive they are as people. They are compassionate and quietly intense. They are committed to developing people and are sensitive truth tellers. They are highly metaphorical and visionary, but they also have the capacity to execute their plans. INFJs are self-confident and individualistic thinkers who are quietly forceful. INFJs are persistent. Keen and industrious, the INFJ builds harmony and brings innovative solutions to pass. INFJs understand people, and as managers, they have an upper hand in knowing their audience.

Conclusion:

Although the 16 fruits or types discussed include great variation, they all originate from the same species family so no matter how insurmountable some differences appear, they are not. In this life, it is impossible for one to operate within their preference 100 percent of the time-- therefore, some point of connection can always be cultivated between the types. In conclusion, the seed of one's personality yields particular fruit and these fruits combine making either a flavorful or distasteful fruit salad. People's willingness to grow and step outside of their preferences when necessary is what makes a good recipe.

About Catherine Farlow:

Catherine Farlow graduated Summa Cum Laude from Pepperdine University, earning a Bachelor of Arts in Creative Writing and minors in Film and Intercultural studies. She notices personality before eye color and is keenly interested in Myers-Briggs typology. Her other passions include film, dance, vegetarianism and Christian faith. Her website is ***www.personalitytyping.weebly.com***

Chapter 4

The Rules of Engagement

By

Desyra Highsmith

It's Monday morning and your employees' alarm clocks are going off throughout the region. For some, the feeling of dread washes over them as they smash the snooze button. They drag themselves out of bed because they know they must. Their lack of motivation and enthusiasm is palpable. It hasn't always been this way. There was a time when they anticipated each work day with an excitement and hopefulness about what they would contribute, learn or accomplish that day. They enjoyed the camaraderie of their colleagues; they actually had fun AND got a lot of work done. But somewhere along the way, all of that changed. You can't help but notice that the enthusiastic employee you interviewed and hired, now drops balls, misses deadlines, runs out the door at the stroke of 5:00pm (or 4:57 when you're not looking), an no longer seems fired up.

What if this could have been avoided? The warning signs of disengagement were there, but missed or just misinterpreted as carelessness, disorganization, lack of motivation, etc. But if we are being truly honest, the likeliest of all possibilities is that the transformation of your once eager employee has something... well, a lot... to do with *you*. I respectfully offer this possibility for your consideration, and implore you to silence the "she's not talking about me" internal dialogue. An overwhelming number of exit interviews and employee morale issues I have had to address emanate from a troubled employee/manager relationship. Surprisingly, as consistent as the cause of the discontent, are the managers' shock and denial that they could have had anything to do with the employees' lackluster performance and negative attitude. Without open mindedness to the power you hold as a manager, and the impact your words and style have on your employees, you may regularly find your employees leaving, or being invited to leave, the organization. It's a venture that yields great benefit if you are committed to looking in the mirror and exploring what you can do differently.

Why you ask? Engaged employees are committed to the organization, more productive and impactful contributors, are less likely to take their talents and experience elsewhere, and provide better customer experiences necessary in the competitive marketplace. A study done by Dale Carnegie and MSW found that 80% of those dissatisfied with their immediate manager or supervisor were disengaged. There is an undeniable correlation between engagement and effective management. Studies also show that more than 70% of all employees are not fully engaged, costing businesses billions of dollars in employee turnover. Those companies with high employee engagement scores far outperform their competitors. With so much clarity and information around the impact of engagement, why aren't more and managers doing something about it? Not to oversimplify, but it truly boils down to two main reasons; (1) they don't know how to spot when their employees are becoming disengaged (2) and they don't realize that they hold much of the power to create or rebuild engagement. Skill, knowledge and experience have very little to do with establishing the connection with your employees that leads to engagement. The skills are not cerebral; they are the human....personal...expressive. You will have to place your technical prowess and analytical proficiency to the side while building the lasting connections with your employees that creates an environment where they enjoy working and contributing.

I recall a manager who was adamant that he wanted to terminate one of his employees that just wasn't getting the job done according to his expectations. It is fair to expect performance and outcomes, so I inquired further for details of "Janice's" shortcomings.

Mr. Manager: "Janice is just not performing. I ask her to do something and she just doesn't get it."

Me: "Is it that she doesn't complete the assignments you give her?

Mr. Manager: "Well, she does them, but it's not the way I want it. She does just what I ask her to do and doesn't go any further.

Me: "Have you discussed this with her? Does she know that she is not meeting your expectations?" What measures have you taken to communicate these performance issues with Janice?"

Mr. Manager: "I think so. I mean I have, sort of. But I think she's just not the one for the role. She just isn't learning the job fast enough."

Me: "If I were to bring her in to discuss this, would this conversation be familiar to her or would she be surprised"

Mr. Manager: "Well she should know." I think it's pretty clear that I'm not happy with her performance." (The danger of assumptions)

In the end I called the employee into my office to hear her manager's performance assessment and, as you might guess, she was surprised. There had been no clear direct communication, or specific feedback that she could use to be more effective. Instead, she just saw the disengaged manager who had basically given up on her and in turn was feeling deflated and lacking confidence. Her manager had the maturity to apologize and give her another chance, this time applying more guidance and recommendations. With greater clarity around expectations she blossomed, and some years later is still working for the same manager with expanded responsibility.

This manager almost lost a great employee because he did not realize **The Golden Rule of Engagement**:

Engage others as you would have others engage you.

You absolutely will see exponential returns if you are engaged and invested in your employees. As I witnesses the exchange between this manager and his employee, I could see that she had not previously experienced such engagement from him prior. He looked her in the eye, he was clear about what she was not doing well, and he listened to her response. She held back tears as she replied to him. She was feeling frustrated by his lack of direction and didn't really understand what exactly he wanted. As her position was entry level in a highly technical department, she relied on him to train and guide her, and he instead left her like a ship without a sail. There was a magical moment of understanding, and even better, there was subsequent investment from both parties. The manager heard her and placed greater effort in her exposure and development. She worked very hard to meet his expectations and grew in her role.

Those moments of engagement, when they occur regularly, build and strengthen relationships and teams and ultimately organizational cultures. Managing humans requires that you recall their humanness. Often managers have a subconscious perception that once their employees report to work they transform into robots; void of the same human desires which drive them outside of the workplace; personal gratification, recognition, security, support, encouragement, appreciation , and the list goes on. Unfortunately, I have witnessed the damaging effects of managers that forget the very simple truth that employees don't leave their inner selves in the parking lot when they come to work. These managers inevitably build toxic environments with employees scrambling for a departmental transfer or to just leave the company when that is not possible.

Their employees are easily spotted because they possess the telltale vacant expression, seem depleted of energy, and just go through the motions; contrary to the energetic, positive achiever they had once been. There are sure characteristics of employees who are breaking away and losing their connection and "fire" to perform. I have seen it happen so many times I can spot a potential casualty as though there was a red laser glowing on their forehead. The manager-employee relationship has the greatest impact on the employee experience, their engagement, their feelings of worth and value as an employee and the satisfaction they receive from their work. Yes, of course there are other factors, but as a manager, your contribution weighs heaviest.

Tuning your attention to employee behavior and recognizing the beginning signs of disengagement will elevate you to new levels of influence and effectiveness as a leader. Creating and sustaining an engaging environment requires equal parts of owning your power to influence the environment and understanding the indicators of the state of your employees' experience in the environment you lead. Is it healthy and thriving? In need of triage and resuscitation? Or is an exorcism or resurrection needed?

I recently held a series of focus groups to learn how individual contributors define management effectiveness, and what characteristic they most value. Far above and beyond knowledge, skills and abilities was respect, concern for their employees, regular clear communication, and the demonstration of a strong work ethic. In sum, ENGAGEMENT. They wanted to know their manager is invested in them, takes time to talk to them, is invested and energized around their work and values their contributions.

To spot the signs is not scientific, psychological or cognitive. You simply need to become a *noticer*. Truly successful managers have mastered the simple art of *noticing*. As simple as that sounds, your own mounting workload, phone calls, e-mails, meetings, personal responsibilities, etc., create a fog in our space that obstructs the visibility of the simplest of things going on around us and desensitizes us to our own behaviors as well. The quicker you are able to notice the signs of disengagement, the sooner you can course correct.

Any Vacancies?

Eyes are truly the windows to the soul. They alone can express the spectrum of emotion, from enchantment, to surprise, to rage and sorrow. So too can they express interest, connection and engagement. A sure sign of fading engagement is the distant glaze in the eyes of the disengaged. If you're not sure exactly what this looks like, rent *Invasion of the Body Snatchers* (1978 film) where human beings were being substituted by emotionless aliens. Often in the workplace, we don't think to look into the eyes of others for signs of their state of mind and emotion, although, we should. Like the indicators on the dashboard of your car, they are the indicators if something is going on internally that needs attention or repair. As a trainer, I trust my read of learner's eyes to determine if they are invested in the learning experience, if they understand the lesson, and if they are responding to the content and delivery. I have learned to become incredibly sensitive at the moment a participant begins to wander in thought, struggle with the concept or worst of all, fight off a good snooze! When you are in front of rooms full of people on a regular basis, where you are responsible for imparting valuable information in a way that will be applied to their performance or transform behaviors, it is critical to maintain capture of attention, interest and connection. All trainers and seasoned managers know that once that is lost, the potential meaningfulness of the experience dissipates with it. It is difficult, yet not impossible to regain once it is noticed.

However, as a manager, you are not in need of momentary attentiveness for a daylong session or even a week. You require consistency in focus, effort, involvement and engagement. You have your own deadlines, projects and goals to meet, so it may not be something you are regularly tuned in to. However, it's a muscle that you need to exercise to ensure your employees are stimulated, engaged, and connected to the outcomes they are responsible for. As important, you must demonstrate the same to them; your eye contact demonstrates an interest and value for what they have to say. When your employees come into your office, do you continue looking towards your monitor and typing away?

Do you look away each time the phone rings to see who is calling or scroll through texts and e-mails on your cell phone? All of these breaks in eye contact communicate to your employees that they are unimportant. On the contrary, if you have had an employee delivering important information and have not broken eye contact, they are getting the message that you value what they have to say and that you appreciate their message at that moment. However, building consistency in this experience is what leads to an interpretation that they are truly valued. Building a sense of value and importance in your employees is like a vaccine for disengagement and it can begin with something as small as eye contact and attentiveness.

When Silence is Not Golden

We all have seen the hungry employee looking to prove themselves and offer their opinions thoughts and insights at each meeting, they ask questions and seek to understand everything! But compare that to your dearly departed employees (in an emotionally detached sense). Have you ever posed open ended questions to your team hoping for a choir of contributions and instead.......crickets? I recall a frustrated leader venting to me about his unmotivated team who wouldn't say anything during department meetings. "At every meeting I ask them if they have any ideas about how we can make things better. They never say a word, and just look like they can't wait for the meeting to end! They don't recommend anything to make our processes more efficient, or improve teamwork...nothing! Their attitudes are so negative." After further exploration, I learned that this manager was known for shooting down the ideas of his employees. Often when he did listen to their ideas, they would disappear into a suggestion abyss, never to be heard about again. Alarmingly, these ideas would occasionally resurface, as his own! Well no wonder he couldn't pry involvement and engagement out of them.

Ironically, silence is the loudest signal that there is something incredibly wrong with the atmosphere. The challenge is being introspective, honest and seeking feedback without defensiveness. This manager fell into the same trap as many do; believing the problem was not *him*. As a leader, it goes with the territory that you must start and end your reflection with exploration of what you are doing to create the situation. Pride has no place in the establishment or repair of any relationship when you think about it. Has hearing the words "I'm sorry" ever instantly returned your blood pressure from boiling to a slow simmer? Have you ever felt a huge weight lifted after facing the music for something you had done wrong and asking for forgiveness? Have you ever found a person endearing because they were completely transparent, allowed flaws and all to be seen by others? Each instance required a decision to trade pride for humility to get the bigger win!

Parking Lot or Indy 500?

If disengagement is truly at a critical stage and your environment is bordering on toxic, 5:00 may more closely represent an evacuation than an end of day departure. In fact, when I am interviewing candidates, I sometime ask the following question:

"If I were in the parking lot at your current (or previous) job at the end of the day, would I be more likely to see the cars departing sporadically over time, or would I risk being run over by employees peeling out of the parking lot? "

If I'm interviewing a potential manager, I can piece together a picture of the engagement of their current team. If I am interviewing an individual contributor, I'll better understand the type of environment they are accustomed to.

If your previously conscientious employee has transformed into a "clock watcher"....beware. At the stroke of quitting time they are at your door saying good night; or worse they just leave without saying anything, this is not an engaged employee. Now I don't mean that your employees should stay regularly for hours after the typical end of day, because if this is the case, you may be losing employees due to burnout rather than disengagement. But it goes without saying, that any employee fully committed to producing outcomes and meeting deadlines will be motivated to put in the extra time where needed to achieve results. Engaged employees care about the quality of the work they produce, they care about the positive feedback received from a job well done, and they care that they are meeting goals and building credibility and building a reputation of dedication, seriousness and commitment. Driven employees leave when the job is done, while disengaged employees are done when it's time to leave.

So in visiting with that man or woman in the mirror, you must ask the reflection if there has been a creative effort to motivate employees around a common goal, a shared purpose, desired outcomes, the certainty of recognition and acknowledgement (more on this later). Remember the Engagement Golden Rule - ***Engage others as you would have others engage you***. Are you nipping at their heels as your employees run out of the door or are you exemplifying the commitment and dedication you want to see in them? Are you demonstrating and generating enthusiasm and excitement around a purpose?

A manager I once knew was the king of the clock watchers. He would virtually leave skid marks as he screeched out of his parking space. At 5:00 his department looked as I imagine it would at 2:30 in the morning; dark, empty and locked. It was no surprise that employees in that department were known for doing the bare minimum and at one point were disciplined for standing next to the exit several minutes before their time to leave, waiting for the clock to advance. Wow! If that isn't disengagement by way of mismanagement, I don't know what is! This particular manager would complain of the mounting workload and the impossibility of accomplishing the many demands of his role. However, it can't be expected to achieve or motivate exceptional outcomes when our efforts and engagement are basic and minimal. He by way of example trained his employees in the same mediocrity and created a department of underachievers. Engagement and excellence is inspired and sustained by the one at the helm.

On the contrary, the electric experience of feeling stoked about a project and reaching towards a goal, a clear purpose....one you can envision...and care about.....That's the makings of engagement. Earlier in my career I worked for record company and had an incredibly enthusiastic, committed manager who was passionate about our work. I can recall working 7 days a week for weeks on end; starting sometimes at 5:00am and continuing well into the night. Even with all that time and energy, it was by far the best work experience I have had to date. I was so engaged I almost couldn't turn my engagement off. Even though it's my character to give 100%, I wasn't just *doing* extra; I was completely plugged in...Engaged to the highest power! The VP inspired zeal and increasing motivation to do more because she was right there with me early mornings, late evenings and weekends. We were a team with a shared purpose. She exercised the Golden Rule of Engagement and the outcome was full throttle engagement in pursuit of a unified purpose.

Wanted: Jugglers

I don't think there is a job in existence that hasn't required more to be done with less. The tough economic times circa 2008 forced companies to become leaner than ever. Cut backs may have started with searching for and cutting any "fat" in spending and staffing. But at some point, financial challenges forced a need to cut into the lean meat and lay off good performing, valuable employees too. Those who remained were called to do their own job and the jobs of those who were let go. Expectations for performance began to change as this need to wear many hats, and keep many balls in the air became the new normal. Now among the top of the list of key competencies for many roles is flexibility. This is code for, "can do more than one job". Cross training became a regular part of training and some onboarding programs to instill this competency. As a manager, you no doubt have been charged with the same responsibility. Gone is the luxury of delegation, and project oversight. Now you too, must get your hands dirty and be fully entrenched in the projects you may have in the past planned, strategized and.....well.....*managed*. Now you have joined the ranks of the "executors" and have your plate full of many varied projects, responsibilities including the more task oriented of responsibilities.

Although your employees likely discuss the insanity of all they are expected to accomplish as one human being, they realize down deep that the story doesn't change drastically elsewhere. They may gather to lick wounds and vent, but they realize the changed landscape of the workplace. However, there are limits and boundaries to what is humanly possible. Unrealistic expectations of a role can be the culprit of balls being dropped, i-s not dotted and t-s not crossed. It is a challenge to be detail oriented when doing the workload of 2-3 individuals. When balls are being dropped regularly this can be a warning sign of an unmanageable workload, performance issues, inefficient processes, or disengagement. When you begin to notice deadlines being missed and errors being made, you must quickly asses what is to blame.

Often I have experienced managers complaining about the work performance of an employee without evaluating cause. It's simple to swoop in and simply criticize performance, reprimand, or terminate an employee for poor results. However, in talking to many employees on the other side of this criticism, they will often express feeling undervalued for their contributions, and slowly begin to disconnect as a result. Many may recall when there was a team to assist a project they now do alone, and are wondering why years later the positions that were eliminated have not been replaced since the recovery. It is human nature to withhold when you are feeling used or taken advantage of. It is not relevant whether this is true or not. The fact that there is a perception that the organization or *you* are taking them for granted will quickly lead to lack of allegiance and trust – and this is a cancer to employee engagement.

Does this mean you have to run out and add headcount to your team to lighten their load? Absolutely not. Simply giving employees whatever they ask for is not reasonable, and may not be required. Your assessment may reveal that adjustments that can be made to process, priorities and work distribution to manage the situation.

However, the most effective way to manage is to first LISTEN. When you notice the balls being dropped, open conversation with the employee "Typically you are very thorough and detail oriented. However, lately there have been a few uncharacteristic errors in your work. Is anything wrong, or is there something I can help you with? "Sincerity is key; you must truly be willing to hear the response. Even if it is a criticism of you. Your goal is to hear the truth so you can manage to it. Without knowing the reality of what is affecting your employees you will not be able to truly address them and prevent disengagement.

How *You* Doin' (sorry I'm from Jersey)

I once knew a manager who tried to rule with an iron fist. His employees did not trust him and felt that he demonstrated favoritism and unfairly disciplined employees for every little error. I had numerous meetings with employees questioning the warnings and suspensions they were being given while others were able to get away with the same behavior without recourse. I wanted to witness his methodologies first hand to understand how it was that his department had become so polluted and disengaged. I observed him talking over his employees and cutting them off to defend himself and discount all they had to say. He tried to force compliance and he wanted to be right more than to understand and fix the root issues. You could literally see them "check out" when he began to talk because he had lost all credibility. They would shake their heads, flash a roll of the eyes out of frustration, and eventually acquiesce and say nothing.

I met with him afterwards and explained to him that his failure to listen to his employees and hear them and engage in a conversation to resolve the issue was causing more damage than whatever errors he thought he was correcting through discipline. He was winning the battles but losing the war. If he heard them, they might be willing to hear him as well. Empathic listening requires you to truly want to first understand the other person before moving in to make your own points understood. After several sessions of coaching he was ready to meet with his entire department of over 70 people, and he actually apologized for his behavior. He was humble, and sincere, and explained how he understood how his methods were causing stress and anxiety in the department and this was not his intention. One of his employees said something I will never forget; "We are willing to do whatever you ask of us, we'll lay down in the corner and die if you ask us to, but please just do it nicely." Wow! That is extreme, and of course that would never be among any manager's request, but it illustrates how deeply employees value respect and being heard and treated fairly.

In this example the employees' feelings about their job and the company were initially soured because of the work of one person. Relationship with direct management is a key driver to employee engagement, and despite how obviously wrong this manager was in his approach, he still had no clue about the effect it was having until he was told. In fact, in most cases, even when the offenses are much milder, the manager will not initially make the connection between their behavior and the results they are getting. It's been said that we measure others by their behaviors and ourselves by our intentions. Somehow we think if we don't intend any harm that this should be enough to ward off any damage. This couldn't be more untrue. Our intentions may be a reflection of our character, but they do not determine others' experience with us. Perhaps you are not a tyrannical leader, but you may have difficulty letting others ever get a word in edgewise, you may be moody, micromanage or be hypercritical. Whatever the issue, be honest with yourself, and be willing to listen to the truth and make the adjustments that could lead to monumental results.

No One Likes to Be Taken For Granted

Acknowledgement and recognition is the outward expression of appreciation. Acknowledgement can be as simple as "Thank You", but it goes a long way. Part of making employees feel valued is acknowledging the small wins throughout the day to day. I make it a point to say thank you every time one of my employees brings me a report, a document, delivers some important information, etc. It's just naturally how I was raised. When someone does something for you just always say thank you. No matter how big or small. That always stuck with me and is a part of my fabric if you will. But it seems that that was not part of everyone's upbringing. For some, the mentality is that you "should" be bringing this to me; after all I'm the boss. What kind of results do you think this gets on the appreciation meter? When it comes to showing respect and appreciation for your employees, make sure the basics exist, or there is nothing to build upon. When you come in to the office, say "Good morning", when you leave say "Good night, have a nice evening", etc. I have actually heard employees complain that they never know when their manager arrives or leaves because he says nothing to them. They perceive this as him thinking he is above it. When this particular manager would be out of the office, he wouldn't tell his team he would be out that day. How easy could it have been to let his team know that he would be out of the office the next day and if they needed him to call him on his cell or that he would not have access to e-mail, etc. whatever the case would be? However, saying nothing made his team feel unworthy of his communication. Failure to acknowledge any person will surely communicate to them that they are invisible to you or unworthy of your attention. Either case will build a chasm between you and your employees that maintains a separation unsupportive of collaboration, synergy and innovation.

Acknowledgement, although basic, communicates to another that they matter. Most every person wants to matter, be seen and valued. Sincerely acknowledging your employees regularly must be as consistently a part of your everyday "must dos" likes remembering your phone or keys and checking your e-mail, it's a human and a business necessity.

When you fail to develop a connection with your employees, they are working for the "company" and not for you; (*insert your here*). When they leave, it will be mostly because of you and not the company, I assure you. There is a level of commitment that employees develop for the corporation, but their true experience and perception of the organization comes from their direct relationship with their manager. The company can develop programs and provided benefits as well as articulate corporate values and principles, however, it relies on its leaders to truly demonstrate these values and make them part of the employee experience. For example; your company can say that they value diversity and the innovation that can result from the coming together with various perspectives, backgrounds and experiences. However, if everyone in your department is a 50 year old male and millennial employees' ideas are regularly rejected because that is "not the way we do it", then all the corporate promoting in the world will not transcend marketed values into a real experience for the employees. These become imbued in the organization when employees HAVE the experience, not when they HEAR that this should be the experience. Recognition is not simply a pat on the back for a job well done, although this too should happen with some regularity. Beyond this, recognition is an active effort to see your employees' points of view and recognize the potential value in each of them. As a leader, you must too be a gold miner. Yes, you may not hit the "big one" but there are priceless nuggets of gold in the thoughts, ideas, and perspectives of your employees. Successful teams rely on synergy; when there exists openness to outcomes that no one had ever expected because there is freedom to entertain the various contributions of the team to create a beautifully unique and unexpected outcome. This can vary from the mundane transformation of a process to the design and development of a new product. It's a challenge for some leaders because you have done "it" for so long, have seen what works and what doesn't and basically would rather charge ahead with instructions and drive execution. But in doing so, you are sacrificing the great for the good. No doubt your good decision, keen instincts and careful execution have brought you into a position of leadership. However, there are new heights of success that can be reached when you build confidence in your team to offer their thoughts and ideas in a safe environment where, whether implemented or not, they're ideas are respected and heard.

Let Creativity Reign

Igniting creativity requires developing environments alive with purpose, made up of individuals concerned with excellence and seeking to do more than expected. The fragility of creating such an environment is learning how to not only recognize as we discussed, but also to delicately decline inclusion of thought contributions that cannot be incorporated into the project, solution, etc. Once an employee feels "shot down" the likelihood that they will continue to contribute or offer their ideas significantly diminishes with each such event. If not careful, you can be sacrificing tons of gold nuggets that that employee will now withhold out of fear, lack of confidence, intimidation, etc., You may not be aware that you are doing this so, among the first things to be considerate of is your facial expressions and your body language. Regardless of what your mouth says, your face can easily read "what the heck are you thinking? There is no way we're doing that!" Looking away, demonstrates loss of interest so maintain eye contact with the employee through their contribution; remember acknowledgement.

Let's say you are planning a product launch at a trade show and one of your employees suggests that there should be pyrotechnics as the new product emerges from a monumental structure. Now you are thinking this will completely blow our budget. Did he not hear the budget discussion? We would have to hire specialists; none of us know anything about pyrotechnics? We could set the whole convention hall on fire. Is he crazy"? As your team discreetly rolls their eyes, and shift in heir seat, this employee would pick up the vibe, probably shut down, and not say too much else. However, if you are a gold miner, you could instead say; "I see you are thinking about something spectacular to really capture peoples' attention and draw them in to know more about the product." Then you can pose some of the thoughts you have in mind as questions back to the employee. Do you have experience with pyrotechnics? "Well, no. " " Do you have any idea how much something like that might cost?" "Well, no." "Ok, well if you can find out some more information about your idea, perhaps we'll know more about what is involved. However, I do like the idea of an impressive display that will outshine the other product launches in the arena. Perhaps if the pyrotechnic idea doesn't pan out, we could create a similar affect with lighting? "

Instead of completely shutting the employee down, you recognized his contribution, gave him the opportunity to explore it further, to perhaps see for himself whether it is worth consideration. You also highlighted the gold nugget in the idea. The idea of flames shooting out in an indoor arena may not be what you had in mind, but the launching the product in a big way is. So by recognizing the valuable aspects of the idea and not focusing in on the negative, you are encouraging future contribution.

Get out of your own way

Do you have preconceived notions of what a manager should be? Do you think that as a leader you should have all the answers? Can never be wrong? Must always be in control? Well a leader should have a good deal of the answers, should maintain composure but most certainly can be wrong and should always be authentic, sincere and real. Employees are watching your every move, so don't think for a moment you can fool them. They know when you are wrong; don't know an answer, etc. They appreciate when you are honest. If you don't know, say you don't know. If you were wrong about something, say you were wrong. Talk about a bang for your buck. These simple acts will build an appreciation in your team faster, deeper and stronger than could ever be developed by always pretending to be right!

I recall a manager who, although very personable funny as a peer, put on an entirely different persona when she was in manager mode. She became stoic; serious, inflexible, and just had to be right about EVERYTHING! It was killing the morale in her department. The team felt that nothing they could say or do would ever be right or enough. She always had a better way and would take them through such lengthy analyses and explanation that they would just give up trying to offer new ideas. This instead of building an environment where people felt challenged to stretch performance, were doing enough to get by. After all, why should they do more? They would just get shot down, criticized.

She was frustrated by the complacency and mediocre performance of her team. Why were they doing just enough? Why were their projects lacking any creativity? Why were they not finding new ways to improve their processes and manage information? These can be complex questions, as there can be a mix of variables; a bad apple in the bunch, performance limitations, etc. But until leadership has been addressed, nothing else can truly be assessed. How do we know if capabilities are lacking if leaders aren't creating environments where the "best of you" can be shared.

Engagement thrives when there is a fearlessness, openness and comfort in contributions. As a leader, it is your responsibility to build such an atmosphere where this can exist. In sum, to build engagement, develop those characteristics and sensitivities that tune you in to others and draw them in to you. It is the soft skill side that will win the quest for engagement. The experience you create for your employees is less about how managerial you can appear and all about how authentically human you are.

About Desyra Highsmith:

Desyra Highsmith currently leads the Human Resources Center of Excellence for Middle Atlantic Products of Legrand, North America. Desyra holds degrees in Psychology and Sociology from Rutgers College in New Brunswick, New Jersey, and a Certification in Human Resources from Farleigh Dickenson University. Additionally, Desyra is a certified Franklin Covey trainer, facilitating courses such as *The 7 Habits of Highly Effective People®* and *Inspiring Trust®,* and is a certified facilitator of the *Myers-Briggs Type Indicator®.* Desyra has taught for various colleges and clients such as Barnes and Noble, 3M and ITT. Out of her training roots in the areas of communication, leadership and professional development has grown a heightened sensitivity to the "human" element impacting learning, engagement and both individual and corporate growth. This keen insight has resulted in the deployment of impactful training programs and the establishment of transformational company cultures where engagement and emotionally intelligent leadership thrive. Her innate passion for building environments where people grow, contribute and maximize capabilities has resulted in dynamic, ever evolving organizational environments with minimal turnover, thriving employee programs, and the regular occurrence of open employee/management exchanges.

Her various leadership roles in Training and Development, Diversity, Employee Programs/Relations and even Recruiting and Benefits have been made successful by building atmospheres for creative collaboration and valued contribution.

Desyra's additional passions include writing and producing original music, writing children's books and assisting displaced workers with their career search. She resides in New Jersey with her daughter Aria.

Chapter 5

Managing a Diverse and Inclusive Workforce

By

Brenda D. Kitchen, MBA

What is our challenge?

I love to have intellectual conversations in my head. I know that the combination of "me, myself and I" are pretty smart and the three of us always come up with the best ideas...Really? So the questions that we are currently deliberating are: Why is it important to have the skills/tools to manage a diverse and inclusive workforce? Isn't it more comfortable to surround myself with people like me and avoid the hassles of diversity?

These are only a few of the questions that could be on the minds of corporate mid-level and senior managers. They may not be topics of conversation, but they are considerations for those who may not have "done the work" to explore their biases and assumptions as it relates to people outside of their group of comfort and self-identity.

Having worked in corporate America for over thirty years, I have found that one theme in business has not changed – treat people with dignity and respect. My experience tells me that even though operating on this principle is good for creating a positive workplace environment, there are many caveats to this message. There are numerous organizations whose espoused theories don't match their theories in use. What do I mean? Managers espouse or talk about the value of dignity, respect, trust, teamwork, integrity and creativity in the workplace. Yet, if you were to have an "off the record" conversation with their employees, you would find that there are behaviors and situations that occur daily that cause people to doubt the sincerity of any of those values. We often find that people are not being treated with dignity and respect nor are they being assessed based on their performance and what they contribute to the organization. Daily, they are being engaged based on the visible and often the not so visible differences that cause them to be identified in a certain group.

When people hear the words "workforce inclusion" or "diversity and inclusion", there is this inquisitive look that often appears on their faces. Some are wondering what those phrases really mean; some are committed to their success in their environments and others struggle with how to work within the confines of workforce inclusion and see success for themselves. The assumption so many times is that if a corporation has a diverse workforce,

- there will not be enough room at the table for the majority
- unqualified minorities will be given jobs that others deserve
- the quota system is alive and well in the workplace

We have allowed myths, half-truths and lies to exist within the discussion of diversity and inclusion and it has become difficult to manage the change in our workplace. It is time to address some of the things that create a negative environment towards diversity and inclusion.

Why is it important to understand Affirmative Action?

One of the first things that many companies cover in orientation of new hires and new managers is the concept of Affirmative Action. The discussion is usually viewed as a "tick mark" item to cover quickly and move on. However, there are many misconceptions about affirmative action that lead to trouble later. When I facilitate diversity workshops, I ask "What is the first thing one thinks about when they hear the words "Affirmative Action?" The response is "quotas" one hundred percent of the time. That tells me that no matter how many times we explain it in our "tick mark" discussions, we have not done an adequate job.

I am amazed that in 2013 we are continuing to have the "I can't find talented minorities" conversation. My reply, "Where are you looking? and What are you looking for?" If your fundamental view is that you are hiring to fill a quota and you think you are over your limit, you won't look or search for the best and the brightest. You'll look for what makes you comfortable. I won't get into a lesson on affirmative action here, but it is important to recognize that it does cover more than people of color. In fact, women have been generously rewarded by the reach of affirmative action. The use of affirmative action principles in companies that do not seek opportunities with the Federal government is voluntary. This is what the majority of people often misunderstand.

What is the meaning of diversity and inclusion?

In the United States we often find that diversity is defined at the extreme base by race and gender. For so many years the US workforce was male dominated, more specifically white male dominated. It is noticeable that over the last twenty-five years that there has been a shift in the way businesses look and operate. As more jobs shift out of the US, technology affects how we do business.

We are attempting to become a global economy. We are making business decisions in real time over the internet, during phone conferences, webcasts, etc. Our business partners have different faces, cultural beliefs, and thoughts that are not like those that heavily influence us in America. Therefore, companies have to evaluate not only who they are doing business with, but who they are hiring. The talent pool is changing and the attitudes that come along with that change are drastically different. Since race and gender are no longer the only driving forces for defining how our organizations will look and operate we must also explore the emerging markets that are important from an economic perspective in terms of who is buying our products. This exploration and strategic planning will determine who we hire and retain in order reflect that customer base.

The political climate in the US has affected the way we cooperate with each other in the workplace. We have become divided in our attitudes along racial, economic and political lines. This makes for a very hostile environment and also impedes the ability of a manager to recruit and add new individuals to the "team". As we have become more focused on technology and our jobs are more "white collar", we have created a much more social environment of work. Our teams are more like fraternities and sororities. During the days of manufacturing, when we actually made something, all one had to do was show up, go to the line and produce their part of the final product. There was much less social interaction. We must recognize that businesses were not created to be social entities. They were created to solve problems and by doing so, create profit. Today, we are constantly meeting, discussing and attempting to come to consensus on moving a project forward. You begin to see teams of people that are comfortable with each other or cliques that exclude people that they are not comfortable with for whatever reason. We fear what is not like us. We are constantly doing teambuilding activities to make sure that people are able to get along and move the objectives forward to completion. However, we are not getting to the source of the problem...biases, assumptions and attitudes that people may or may not be aware exist. Albert Einstein is quoted as saying: "You can't solve a problem with the same mind that created it." The value of diverse thinking is the difference in viewpoint and we must have diverse thinking for success.

What is the economic impact?

When we take our biases, assumptions and stereotypes to the marketplace we must be aware that there is an economic component to diversity and inclusion.

The Selig Center for Economic Growth provides data on the multicultural economy that is helpful in understanding the importance of valuing the buying power of minorities. Because of the media's portrayal of minorities as poor, criminal, unlearned, on and on, those attitudes show up in the workplace. Even during the presidential race of 2012, the "47 Percent" comment made by Mitt Romney certainly gave us insight into how a person who claims to want to represent the entire US can dismiss such a large portion of the people he or she should be representing.

In 2005, the Pew Research Center did research that outlined detailing the projected changes in the US population by 2050. The one area that seemed to gain the most focus was the fact that: "The non-Hispanic white population will increase more slowly than other racial and ethnic groups; whites will become a minority (47%) by 2050." Jeffrey Passel and D'Vera Cohn wrote a summary of this information that was released in February 2008.

As I began to share this in diversity workshops, I began to notice the level of discomfort in the room with the majority members of the class. I also began to pay attention to the shift in the rhetoric in the national media, especially in politics. The undercurrent of this information was changing the landscape in corporate America on how businesses operate. Even though the senior management was pushing workforce inclusion, the "feeling" in the trenches was that opportunities were going away for the majority community and unqualified minorities would have an underserved ranking in the business arena. It is true that perception is reality. Regardless of the fact that there is a push to operate in a more global economy and to do business with people who don't look like, think like or live like we do as Americans, we want to operate with a sense of control. We want the money, but the partnership...not so much.

The emerging markets in the US are primarily African Americans, Asians, Hispanics, Disabled, Women and GLBT. When you consider the economic impact of doing business with these markets as a whole, there is over $4.5 trillion in disposal income available for investment in the marketplace. The bigger picture is that these groups offer a pool of diverse talent and resources to assist in navigating doing business in diverse markets. During executive coaching sessions, I ask if senior leaders are willing to leave money on the table in their businesses in order to hide or avoid their discomfort with diversity. The answer is usually a resounding no, but the discomfort with the work that will be required to make consistent change is a challenge that many find extremely difficult. They realize that it is the right thing to do, but doing what is right is not always easy.

What is "The Work"?

There is a requirement for exploration of one's beliefs, assumptions and biases in order to be truthful about how we interact with others. In order to achieve organizational inclusion and acceptance, one must understand that change in attitude is a must. There are several prevailing attitudes in the workforce that prevent diversity and inclusion. One is that only those who fit into the traditional values and beliefs will succeed. The attitude of sameness and resistance to cultural change are breeding grounds for negative consequences. A leader/manager in this environment must explore where these attitudes of prejudice and discrimination originate and their impact on self, target and the organization. One of the best examples of this exploration is Jane Elliott's Brown-eyes / Blue-eyes experiment.

In the 1960s, America was a country divided. The black civil rights movement had swept across the country, and as more and more African Americans fought for equality, many racists fought against them.

In the midst of the civil rights movement, Jane Elliott, a white teacher from a mostly white town in Iowa, wanted to be involved in gaining equality for all men and women, regardless of race. Ms. Elliott watched the media coverage of the assassination of Dr. Martin Luther King Jr., and felt appalled by the way the white reporters could not seem to understand what the black community was going through. Elliott realized that the problem was the disconnection between what whites knew about racism and what blacks experienced. So, Elliott developed an exercise to change the way her white students thought about racism.

The Blue Eyes/Brown Eyes Exercise

One morning after King's assassination, Elliott informed her class that they were going to change the way things were done. Blue-eyed children were given pride of place in the classroom. They were given extra recess time, a second helping of food at lunch, and they were allowed to sit at the front of the classroom and participate in class discussions.

Brown-eyed children, meanwhile, were forced to sit at the back of the class and were more severely reprimanded for the same type of behavior that blue-eyed children got away with. Elliott even made up a scientific 'fact' that the melanin that caused blue eyes had been found to be linked with a higher intelligence.

The results were stunning. By the end of the day, the blue-eyed children viciously put down the brown-eyed children. Not only that, but the quiet, struggling blue-eyed students did much better on class assignments, and the louder, successful brown-eyed students did not do as well.

The next day, Elliott reversed the exercise, promoting brown eyes as better than blue eyes. Much of the same results happened, though the brown-eyed students didn't taunt their blue-eyed classmates quite as viciously. By the end of the second day, when the exercise ended, the blue-eyed and brown-eyed children hugged and cried with each other. A class of all-white students had learned what racism felt like.

The fact that an elementary teacher could expose the feelings of racism with this experiment is phenomenal. For me, this exposes so many stereotypes that still exist. The belief that the majority is smarter, that assimilation is required and is therefore successful; that by virtue of the color one entered the world with automatically escalates them to priority status on earth is mind boggling.

This exercise is a great start for opening the conversations around race, gender, sexual preference and the other social issues that face our society today. However, I think it is important to understand that the group that is being targeted with bias and stereotypes walks this life daily. An exercise for those who oppress only gives you a snap shot in time experience. One must become consciously competent to their belief, attitudes and behaviors.

Another requirement is to explore if you as a leader/manager do the token inclusion in order to appear to be open to differences, but your beliefs, values and behaviors don't change. This shows up as hiring someone who is different from the rest of your team, they stay a short while and your excuse for their exit is that they didn't have the skills, drive or motivation to be successful. Even worse, they could be stereotyped as trouble-makers for their commitment to diversity and trying to open the door for others in the company. Your behavior makes it difficult for them to be successful because you cannot see the obstacles you put in their way to prevent them from becoming fully integrated into your organization.

You may reach a point where your numbers are representative of diverse employees and imply that your organization is inclusive in its practices for the best and brightest talent. However, the numbers alone don't overcome the individual barriers to inclusion. Those barriers include your beliefs about groups that differ from the majority, be they real, myth or lie. Perceptions become reality and the minority is fighting against a force that they may not realize or recognize, but know is present.

Your goal is to be about diversity and inclusion because it adds value to your organization. It is part of your fiber and you are no longer explaining or making a case for it. When you reach this point, numbers are not an issue. Best talent is the driving force.

One important point that should be addressed is the assumption that all minorities are unqualified or that their qualifications must be explained to the majority members who are interested in the same position when a minority is hired. Another is that if a minority gets a job, the majority loses.

For many years, I facilitated diversity workshops in the hospitality industry for a well-respected leader in the industry. Their motto was: "Diversity is the right thing to do." This always impressed me because it was a top-down approach to diversity and inclusion in this company and had been standard operating procedure for many years. Their approach forced not only their leadership, but every employee to take a long hard look at their own thoughts, beliefs, prejudices and biases and how they came to believe what they believe about those who are not like them.

Diversity has an economic component and truly affects the bottom line of any business. When the boundaries of inclusion expand from race and gender to include religious, disability, GLBT, ethnicity, generational, immigration and work life balance issues, corporate leaders will begin the journey to understanding how their focus on diversity must transcend across culture in order to avoid alienation of a group that provides great economic impact for your business. The emerging markets of women, Hispanics, people of color, etc., must be represented not only in the customer/client base, but in every area of the function and level of the business.

There has been a continued push back from some leaders that even though their corporate philosophy is to have a diverse representation in their companies, they have been challenged to find talented, qualified individuals to hire. As a person of color, my translation of that statement is "I have difficulty finding a person who is different but makes me comfortable."

What do we need to do to change?

Managing change is a monumental task.

When you look at emerging markets in our economy, businesses are dependent on more than one demographic segment, but continue to treat people with disrespect. The research shows that the disposable income of African Americans, Hispanics, Asians, GLBT, Disabled and Women has great financial impact on the economy. Yet, these groups are not adequately represented in the upper levels of management in business today. The glass ceiling is not just an idea, it is a reality.

It is my belief that we cannot put the burden of change on the backs of employees. I believe that the head leads the body or sets the tone for the organization. Without a strong executive leadership position for diversity and inclusion, there will be no change and the environment will be toxic.

There are many tools to assist people in their awareness on diversity. I have used the Diversity Awareness Profile (DAP) and know that many of us are Diversity Change Agents, willing to call out wrong when we see it and stand for what is right in our daily lives. Yet, there are the Avoiders who will go along to get along in fear of losing their job and friends. There are also the Perpetuators who know better but join in with those who bully and oppose those who are not like themselves.

How does change management impact our success?

Are the CEOs of major corporations thinking about the changes that need to be made to accommodate a changing workforce? One key question that needs to be answered: "To what extent do you plan to change your people strategy over the next 12 months?"

This question requires that managers / leaders consider their strategies for engaging a wide range of demographics that differ from the current Boomer leadership. When you begin to recognize the differences in generational thinking, you have more creative space to make decisions. The key to unleashing this power is to recognize and engage the wide variety of workers who can bring to the table a vast array of talents, skills and ideas. That means expanding the reach of diversity, upping the degree of inclusion, and using flexibility to bring the pieces together as a dynamic and unified force.

A tool or an attitude?

I believe that there are at minimum, three areas of importance for a manager to focus on to be successful in managing a diverse workforce.

1. Be aware.

    A leader who is not aware of their own bias, stereotypes and assumptions will walk in ignorance, judgment and short-sightedness. Generally speaking, what you dislike most will show up in your life to cause you to deal with your prejudices. When you are constantly facing situations with people that make you uncomfortable, ask yourself "What is it about me that would cause this to be repeated in my life?" Now it's time to work on that issue and resolve it so that it does not cause you to be ineffective in the future.

2. Understanding your own biases, stereotypes and assumptions.

If you don't know what your attitudes are they will be quiet destroyers in your environment. What do I mean? If you have a bias or assumptions about a group that is different from you, there will eventually be a challenge in your ability to recruit the best and brightest talent. The talent that you do lead will certainly be aware of your biased behavior regardless of your lack of recognition. One of the most costly areas of revenue in business is talent retention / turnover. Finding ways to more deeply engage this talent pool can alleviate concerns about finding the right people with the right skills. Turnover is a costly enterprise. Employers have continued to spend more dollars per hire, with a recent increase of more than 25%, bringing the average per-hire cost to more than $3,300. This number is significantly larger for knowledge workers. Turnover costs represent more than 12% of pre-tax income for the average company and up to 40% of earnings for companies at the higher end of the spectrum. Research shows that deeper employee engagement is related to improved retention, customer loyalty, revenue, sales, and profit. Make sure that you are not contributing to the high turnover in your business due to biased behavior.

3. Challenge where your attitudes originate and why you continue to use them as a basis for your beliefs.

When we are inundated with information and it becomes the foundation of our belief system, we tend not to challenge those beliefs going forward. Explore your core beliefs and make the efforts to walk in another's shoes before you assume that your way is the only way. Be a broader thinker and your actions will reflect an attitude of openness and a willingness to change.

About Brenda Kitchen:

Brenda is a management consultant who specializes in facilitation, change management, organizational development and coaching. Her areas of expertise include instructional design, adult learning styles and techniques, styles of communication, change management, organizational behavior, and cross-cultural training, specifically economic diversity management design and implementation.

Brenda has a Bachelor's degree in Psychology from Queens University and a MBA with an emphasis in Business Management from Strayer University. For the past 18 years she has served as the Managing Partner of Vision Resource Management in Charlotte, North Carolina.

Brenda believes that strong communication skills and the ability to build strong relationships are invaluable in the journey towards diverse thought and actions. A diverse attitude is a choice and a work in progress.

Chapter 6

A Tale of Four Coaches
By

SC Matheny

Management has been defined in many ways. It can mean supervising or guiding a group of people to a desired end. It involves systems and resources and is ultimately about producing results. This, of course, makes sense to anyone who is familiar with the topic. Whether someone is a shift manager at the local mini-mart or part of an upper-management team in a multinational corporation, management is about engaging and empowering people, the most valuable resource, to succeed.

My understanding of management and leadership comes predominantly from the fields, courts, gridirons, and rinks of America. I have been involved in sports since I was in elementary school in Orange County, California, with the South Sunrise Little League. I had coaches that could convince their players to run through a brick wall for them. I had other coaches that couldn't convince a parched person in the desert to accept free lemonade. For some of us, our earliest examples of how to lead and manage others were parents, teachers, or troop leaders. I understood management and leadership in terms of coaching. Coaches guided people, managed resources, and got results. Management IS coaching.

Coaches come in many shapes and sizes. Some only speak when they see mistakes. Others are like cheerleaders who never seem to run out of compliments. Some expect perfection. Others are satisfied with great efforts. Sadly, the worst just don't seem to care either way. As a parent of a teen who has played sports for years, I have seen it all. I remember the first time I saw my daughter play softball for a certain coach. Before she came to bat, he said, "Come on, I believe in YOU!" I thought he was very encouraging. This coach was going to be especially supportive of my daughter and bring out the best in her. As the game progressed, I realized that he said this to every girl as she came to bat. "Come on, I believe in YOU!" Game after game, it was the same. Parents started mimicking his patented line. The poor coach lost his team early on because he did not vary his tune. What seemed to be so encouraging had become trite and overused. Coaching can be very frustrating.

As a former chaplain in the National Football League, I experienced four coaches who could not have been more different. From 1995-2005, the Jets went from the bottom of the barrel to consistent playoff contenders. Four coaches guided the franchise from great ignominy to respectability. Each had his style and experienced various levels of success. Through it all, I kept mental notes. The NFL is one of the most highly competitive businesses in the world. Each year the League crowns one winner and has a host of also-rans. Millions of people evaluate a team's performance in real time. The League is about winning and losing, and losers don't stick around long. Good coaching is at a premium. Highly talented teams with poor coaching do not win. Teams with average talent and superior coaching can win it all. This was never so true during my time in The Big Apple.

The Disengaged Coach Equals Disaster

In the spring of 1995, the New York Jets selected Kyle Brady in the first round of the NFL Draft. Kyle was a star. He stood 6'6" and weighed 270 pounds. He was sculpted like a Greek god. He had won All-America honors at Penn State and had helped lead the Nittany Lions to the Rose Bowl. The Jets saw him as an answer to their problems at the tight end position. He could block, run, and catch and was fundamentally sound. He was a good guy, a young man of good character.

At the time, the Jets' head coach and general manager was Rich Kotite. Coach Kotite was a former player who had come to the Jets after a successful four-year stint coaching the Philadelphia Eagles. Kotite led the Jets to a 4-28 record over two seasons. The 1995-96 seasons were unmitigated disasters. There is really no other way to put it. The team stunk, and Kotite was responsible. The Jets' ship was rudderless, floating amidst a sea of mishandled drafts, lack of accountability, and a captain who was disengaged.

Kyle Brady felt the brunt of this mismanagement. Jets fans at Radio City Music Hall had booed Brady when he was selected. Evidently, the fans felt that drafting future Hall-of-Famer Warren Sapp would have been a better choice since the Jets had just drafted tight end Johnny Mitchell a few years earlier, supposedly to fill the position for years to come. Despite the welcome, Brady reported to camp in shape and ready to contribute, but it seemed the commitment was not mutual. Kotite and the Jets had failed to provide Brady and his fellow tight ends a position coach. Brady's position required pass catching ability and blocking skills, so the Jets' figured that he could work with the offensive line coach to perfect his blocking and with the receiving team to help him run routes and catch passes. In reality, the position required one coach dedicated to managing each aspect, which was commonly understood in the League. The team and Kyle suffered because of this oversight.

When the Jets opened the 1995 season at Joe Robbie Stadium in Miami to face the Dolphins, Brady was not confident that he knew his responsibilities for each play. Think about it. This was a first-round draft pick (paid first-round draft pick money) that had not been assigned a position coach! Evidently Brady was not the only Jet that was confused. The team lost 52-14 on that hot September day in South Florida. The Jets won a league worst three games that season because of the way the team was mismanaged and unprepared. Many of the losses were late in the game. This was not surprising. The team was not in shape. Many of its players were overweight and not accountable for working out. Reports circulated that players simply walked in the weight room, signed off that they had worked out, and left. Linebackers that were supposed to weigh 245 pounds had ballooned to nearly 300 pounds. They would simply run out of gas. The head coach was disengaged. There was little accountability for understanding key systems and schemes and the players were not prepared mentally or physically for their responsibilities.

The next season got worse. The team only won ONE game! The Jets had some talented players. For the first part of the season, Neil O'Donnell was their quarterback.

O'Donnell had led the Pittsburgh Steelers to the Super Bowl the year before and was in the middle of a successful career. Yet, he didn't manage to win a game in his six starts before suffering a shoulder injury. And why was this? The team was simply mismanaged from the very start. Talent is not enough. Every team has talent. When the head coach fails to provide much-needed leadership, everything falls apart. Professional football teams are complex entities that require exceptional management to thrive. Coaches must engage and empower their personnel to compete at a high level. While micromanagement can have its pitfalls, disengagement almost always falls flat. This cautionary tale reminds all managers to diligently oversee their responsibilities. While delegation is critical to overall success, a manager must always keep a finger on the pulse of the organization and an eye on the goal.

An Engaged Coach Equals Success

Bill Parcells will be inducted into the Pro Football Hall of Fame in August of 2013. The honor is well deserved. He won multiple Super Bowls and turned moribund franchises into winning organizations. One of his "projects" was the New York Jets. After the disaster that was the "Rich Kotite era" in New York, Coach Parcells restored dignity to the team. The Jets became a respectable opponent immediately after Parcells took the helm.

The late owner of the Jets, Leon Hess, was able to woo Coach Parcells from the New England Patriots in 1997. Parcells' Patriots had been in the Super Bowl the year before and this coaching change for the Jets was seen as a coup of monumental proportions. During Parcells' first year in New York, the Jets were 9-7 and missed the playoffs by one game. This was accomplished with essentially the same team that had gone 1-15 under Kotite the year before. How did this happen? The answer was simple; the coach was completely engaged. Parcells had his finger in the pie. Parcells hired a new strength and conditioning coach who held players accountable to their weight goals and work out plans. Parcells hired assistant coaches that would help manage every level of the team. These assistants were well-qualified and knew what it meant to do things "Bill's way." There was NO other way.

Coach Parcells' Jets won their division in 1998 and were on their way to the Super Bowl that season until John Elway's Broncos took control of the second half of the American Football Conference Championship in January 1999. The Jets had gone from perennial loser to instant winner because of the way one man managed his team. Parcells was appropriately engaged with his organization. He did not micromanage; neither did he disappear when his leadership was required.

Players respected Parcells because he treated them as individuals. He didn't treat everyone the same, but he treated them fairly. Coach knew that while the stick might motivate one player, the carrot was better for another. He got the best out of his team and the organization because he knew how to appropriately engaged his coaches, players and the administrative staff. He was NOT everyone's buddy; yet, he found a way to make each person give his best. He was engaged, but not intertwined, with those under his authority. He brought in talented players, such as Curtis Martin, Vinny Testaverde, and Kevin Mawae, and maximized their abilities. His coaching staff included masterminds, such as coordinators Bill Belichick and Charlie Weis and each position had a coach.

The Jets became a force in the League. Yet, Parcells never took his foot off the pedal. He continued to push. Success didn't spoil him. The team was poised for a Super Bowl run in 1999. Much of the press had labeled the team as the favorite to go to the big game. That ended in the first half of the first game when Jets' Pro Bowl quarterback, Vinny Testaverde, tore his Achilles tendon and was out for the season. Teams that lose their star quarterbacks rarely succeed. The Jets fought valiantly that year but failed to make the playoffs. Coach Parcells decided to retire soon after the season (although his retirement was short-lived as he coached in Dallas a few years later).

Coach Parcells brought a special blend of appropriate engagement and delegation to the franchise. Everyone became accountable for excellence. Yet, it was not based on being under Bill's thumb but under his watchful eye. Many of his assistant coaches went on to be successful head coaches in the NFL or in college football. Parcells picked subordinates well and then let them coach. Parcells held everyone to a high standard, including himself. Great managers spend more time selecting their employees on the front end, so they don't need to micromanage on the backend. They change the culture of their organizations.

The Stubborn Coach Leads to Dissention

When Coach Parcells decided to retire shortly after the 1999 season, the Jets thought that they had their man for the foreseeable future. Bill Belichick, the Jets Defensive Coordinator, had previously agreed to be the coach-in-waiting should Parcells give up his post. Belichick's tenure as head coach of the Jets was short lived as he was wooed by the New England Patriots to be their head coach.

If turnabout is fair play, then this seemed like justice when one considers how Parcells came to the Jets. While Belichick jetted of for Foxboro, Massachusetts, the Jets were once again searching for a coach to take them to the Promised Land. Jet owner Woody Johnson turned again to Parcells' staff and hired linebacker coach Al Groh to run the team.

Initially, Coach Groh was pleasant and positive. He was well read and seemed to have a plan. Under his tutelage, the Jets started out strongly with a 6-1 record. Early in the 2000 season, the New York Jets were known for their miraculous comebacks and spirited play. Vinny Testaverde was back and playing well, and the team seemed destined for the playoffs and a Super Bowl run. Then the wheels fell off. The team lost six of its last nine games and was eliminated from playoff contention on the last game of the season. A glorious September was all but forgotten during the December collapse.

Coach Groh lost control of his team midway through the season. Players complained about the length of team meetings. Coach Groh would try to inspire his team with long-winded stories about The America's Cup races and other illustrations to which his players could not relate. There was a significant disconnect, and when key team leaders approached Groh about their issues, the players were rebuffed and shut out. This rift between the head coach and his star players became media fodder in New York. Groh was set in his ways, and this led to dissention that affected how things played out on the field. He was perceived by his players to be pouting.

I personally felt the sting of Coach Groh's ways. He had told me face-to-face that I would be extended the same courtesies regarding player access that Coach Parcells had given me. Yet, without explanation, I was banned from the team locker room midway through the 2000 season. Rumor had it that one of the players had brought his family in the player's lounge, and such a thing was not acceptable to him. As a result, all non-essential personnel were persona non grata in the locker room at the practice facility. No explanations, no communication, just missives from above without a logical reason. The players saw this behavior and began attributing it to immaturity and emotional issues.

The Jets sat at 9-6 on December 24, 2000. The last game of the season in Baltimore would determine whether the team would make the playoffs or see the once-promising season fizzle out to nothing. The team took a 14-0 lead over that season's champion Ravens, but this time, the shoe was on the other foot. The Jets found a way to give away the game on turnovers and a long punt return. The Jets had 22 first downs to the Ravens 5 and had outgained Baltimore 523-142 in yardage, but six turnovers sealed the team's fate.

On the train ride home, I was responsible for giving the coaches a videotape of the game. I was pretty sure none of them would be interested in watching it, but nonetheless, I was doing my job to offer it to them. As I left the dining car and approached the coaches' car, I saw what I thought to be a strange sight. In that area between cars stood Coach Groh, by himself, slumped against the wall in tears. He was overcome with emotion, which was understandable. However, it spoke to greater issues with his management of the team. He let his personal feelings affect decisions and key relationships. This caused division and was a critical distraction for the team. Groh spent only that one year as the head coach and left to coach at his alma mater, the University of Virginia.

Good coaches must manage their people with balance and openness. They must be willing to listen to their key performers and adjust the way they lead apart from their personal feelings. Managing people is not an easy task, but it is nearly impossible when emotions and stubbornness cloud judgment. Good managers are willing to subordinate their personal feelings for the sake of the team and the greater good of their organization.

The "Buddy" Coach Leads to Disappointment

Herman Edwards was universally liked as a player. He was an undrafted free agent and a solid professional for years with the Philadelphia Eagles and Los Angeles Rams. After his playing days, he became an assistant coach under Tony Dungy in Tampa. He was charismatic, outgoing, and well spoken. He had the fire of a southern preacher, and his energy was contagious. He coached the Jets from 2001-2005. He was a welcome departure from stoic, Coach Groh. Coach Edwards was a "player's coach," which meant that he understood what players wanted and needed from coaches because he had played the game.

Coach Edwards gave the players more freedom than they had been given under the previous two coaches. They were able to handle these liberties because, by and large, they were men who had been drafted or signed by Bill Parcells. They were disciplined and focused. Edwards trusted their strong work ethic. The Jets played well under Herm's leadership. The team won their division in 2002 and made the playoffs on two other occasions. Coach Edwards rewarded his teams with more liberties, which their accomplishments warranted. He became a mentor to players who needed more guidance and direction. He paid special attention to the younger guys and, at times, was more father figure than coach. While this was certainly admirable, it would become his downfall.

One by one, players who had been picked and coached under Bill Parcells retired, were lost to free agency, or were released. The liberties afforded by Coach Edwards had become a liability to the team. Players had begun to believe that Herm had favorites that had a different set of rules. Herm was a defensive coach and many players felt that he was giving "his guys" preferential treatment. Offensive players complained that Coach Edwards allowed his defensive players to sit around on the grass during practice while other players were expected to stand. It became apparent that he was losing control of his team because he had become too close to those under his authority. "Buddy" coaches subject themselves to conflicts of interest and charges of favoritism. While Coach Edwards' heart was in the right place, his ability to manage his team suffered.

Coaching involves making decisions that can affect others adversely. Managing personnel brings the same. Herm crossed the line from being friendly to being friends and it clouded his judgment. He didn't enforce discipline and his players slacked off. By the end of his tenure with the Jets, the team was floundering. Much of this can be attributed to "Buddy" coaching. People pleasing can destroy the team dynamic needed to succeed in any business or organization. It is critical to set up appropriate boundaries with subordinates. People are looking for their bosses to be bosses and not their buddies.

Conclusion

A critical component of management is the ability to coach others. Coaching involves guiding, shaping, teaching, and motivating. Coaches need to be able to make the difficult decisions irrespective of personal feelings and preferences. They must be able to hold others accountable and bring order. From 1995-2005, the New York Jets had coaches who alternated from being poor managers who lost to successful managers who won. Poor coaching led directly to poor play and poor results. Proper levels of engagement were critical to coaching success. Too much engagement weakened and led to favoritism. Too little engagement led to a lack of accountability and misunderstanding. Coach Parcells got it right, and that is why he will be enshrined in the Hall of Fame in Canton, Ohio. I will never forget Coach Parcells. He was a manager extraordinaire.

About SC Matheny:

Scott Matheny spent eleven seasons serving as the Chaplain for the New York Jets from 1995-2005. He experienced first-hand the best and worst in leadership in one of the most competitive businesses in the world, the National Football League.

From the lows of a one-win season to the exhilaration of the American Football Conference Championship Game, Scott had a front row seat to watch great leaders succeed and less capable ones struggle. From regular season pretenders to regular playoff contenders, Scott witnessed the transformation of a moribund franchise to one that garnered respect throughout the League and won. This metamorphosis was the result of changes in both leadership philosophy and its practical implementation.

Scott brings a unique perspective to the subject of leadership and offers an insider's view of how these men and their teams experienced success or failed based on how they are guided and directed. Great leadership made the difference.

Scott is available for keynote speaking and interactive workshops. You can reach him at:

www.scmatheny.com

Chapter 7

The Seven Deadly Sinners:
How to Deal with the Most Difficult People on the
Planet
By

Malcolm O. Munro

Who are the "7 Deadly Sinners" all of us have to deal with? To help us, I've decided to frame our difficult people inside the parameters given in ancient religious texts.

In the late 6th century, Pope Gregory the Great fine-tuned a traditional list of grave offenses into seven items. According to traditions, violations of these areas result in doing time in the "other place" in a whole host of awful tortures. Wise individuals would recognize the penalties for these offenses and hopefully work to avoid doing them. The "7 Deadly Sins" are as follows:

1. **Pride** – The excessive belief in one's own abilities, that interferes with the individual's recognition of the grace of God. It has been called the sin from which all others arise. Pride is also known by its other name: Vanity.

2. **Envy** - The desire for others' traits, status, abilities, or situation.

3. **Gluttony** - An inordinate desire to consume more than that which one requires.

4. **Lust** - An inordinate craving for the pleasures of the body.

5. **Anger** – Anger is manifested in the individual who spurns love and opts instead for fury. It is also known as Wrath.

6. **Greed** - The desire for material wealth or gain, ignoring the realm of the spiritual. It is also called Avarice or Covetousness.

7. **Sloth** - The avoidance of physical or spiritual work.

Now the interesting thing is that even without the religious context, these offenses are really offensive and most of us experience co-workers and bosses who exhibit the behaviors. We need some strategies to deal with them. In this chapter I'll break down each of these into a modern interpretation and introduce techniques on how to work effectively with them. I'm convinced that recognizing and addressing these behaviors will make us more effective as bosses and co-workers. It's a new (and old) way of learning good People Skills!

Deadly Sin #1: Pride

Pope Gregory defined pride as the excessive belief in one's own abilities that interferes with the individual's recognition of the grace of God. It's also often referred to as the sin from which all others arise. Pride is also known as Vanity. I like to call it arrogance.

In my book *12 Simple (but not simplistic) Principles Every Manager Needs to Know*, I made the suggestion to be confident, but never arrogant. Pride is a direct violation of that.

In the workplace, few people are more annoying that arrogant people. I know this because my career path has taken me through the territory where some of these folks tend to work – health care, the military, law, and the senior executive circles in large corporations. Now in all fairness, the folks in these areas worked very hard to get where they are. There's no problem with celebrating achievement and looking for accolades, but at some point they need to get down to business and forget the notion that it's all about them.

Arrogant people exhibit the following behaviors:

- A sense of entitlement

- A confident air about them that never ends
- An incessant string of comments about how great they are
- An arrogant attitude that demeans others of lower rank or position
- A focus on their needs over the needs of others
- Too good to clean up after themselves

I know there are many more, and you probably have a list of your own, but this is a start. Now for some quick strategies on how to deal with them:

Don't:

- Openly confront them – they would enjoy beating you down
- Try to one-up them – this is their game and they know how to play it
- Attempt to compete with them – why bother? It's a losing game

Do:

- Ignore them – they thrive on an audience and accolades – a silent or non-existent audience completely deflates them!

Now it won't work every time, and if you work side by side with these folks it's a daily battle, but the secret to dealing with any difficult person is to do the opposite of what they are looking for.

Pride wants applause and praise. Reward it with silence.

...and if the strategy works for you, don't brag – you might just become what you can't stand! rather than the outward appearance?

Deadly Sin #2: Envy

Pope Gregory defined envy as the desire for others' traits, status, abilities, or situations. There's not a whole lot you can do to make people un-envious of you and even if they are, it won't necessarily ruin your day, so let's view envy from a different perspective...our own.

Living in a country where affluence abounds makes it pretty easy to get caught up in the trap of materialism. Most of us have what we need to live on and more. With our basic needs met, it's often common to then get caught up in what I want, and some envy of what others have. Let me give you an example.

John is a long time employee at XYZ Corporation. His annual salary is 75K with great benefits. His latest review was outstanding and he's extremely pleased with his progress and his status at the company. His salary is great too – far better than what most of his colleagues at other companies are making. John particularly enjoys working with his new team member Sally, a hard-charging and extremely helpful associate who recently came over from one of XYZ's competitors.

One day during a conversation over lunch, Sally lets it slip that her salary is 77K with a bonus plan. John is shocked – Sally has a bonus plan and higher salary? It's not fair.

Suddenly, John's arrangement is just not adequate. How in the world can some newbie who doesn't have half of his talent or work even a fraction as hard get more money and a bonus? John's bitterness and anger eventually affects his performance and team spirit. A rift arises between him and Sally. Within a year, John's annual performance review slips and he eventually leaves XYZ in a fit of anger.

It's a sad story isn't it? Unfortunately, it's pretty common.

Envy is destructive to ourselves, our families, and our co-workers. If left unchecked, it will drive us into depression and debt. Fortunately, there are a couple of strategies that can keep all of us on track and out of the grasp of this "deadly sin."

Don't:

- Compare your salary, benefits, and performance with others. What they make and do is none of your business.
- Get caught up in one-upmanship. Compete against yourself – you're your own worthy opponent.
- Get angry when your co-worker out-performs you. Keep the team's performance as your goal.

Do:

- Be grateful for what YOU have!
- Be gracious when others out-perform you.
- Celebrate someone else's accomplishments – compliment them on their new suit, car, gadgets, etc.

Regardless of where you are or what situation you're in, there is still SOMETHING for you to be thankful for.

Why not take some time right now and think about 10 things you have that others may not. Then say thanks! It's the ultimate cure for the deadly sin of envy.

Deadly Sin #3: Gluttony

Pope Gregory defined gluttony as an inordinate desire to consume more than that which one requires. Now we probably think about this as a food or alcohol issue, but in the workplace I'd like to think about it as a plea for inordinate power or recognition.

Have you ever worked with someone who continually "hogs" all the interesting assignments or duties? They continually volunteer for all the choice jobs and rather than take them on to do them well, they simply want to pride themselves on their massive responsibilities, collecting them as if they were rare baseball cards.

When I was in the Navy, we of course had our regular jobs for which we were assigned and trained, but we also had our choice (sometimes a forced choice) of what were called collateral duties. These "extra" jobs were necessary for the effective running of the operation and many of them were high profile, which enhanced an individual's chances at promotion. In nearly every command I was assigned, there was always one individual who tried to volunteer for as many collaterals as possible with the hopes of course of a higher performance appraisal. Two things always resulted.

1. The collaterals were done at a marginal, unremarkable level

2. The primary job was neglected in favor of the now unmanageable level of collaterals.

Neither result is good. The purpose is lost in an attempt to consume more than is actually required or possible.

So what can you do about the glutton?

Nothing. That is if you're wondering how to change the gluttons around you. People aren't particularly interested in having YOU change THEM. More importantly, how can we prevent ourselves from this workplace gluttony?

Don't:

- Get into the mindset that more is better – think quality over quantity.
- Get caught up in the one-upmanship. Volunteering for extra assignments simply to look

more significant than a co-worker defeats the purpose.

- Overload yourself and expect your hangdog look of overwork to impress your boss. Devote your energy into your main job and let that effort speak for your work ethic.

When we're in the middle of the Holiday season, most of us over-indulge in everything from eating to spending. Gluttony that abounds then only leads to remorse and unachievable resolutions after the first of the year. It's become a holiday ritual that, try as we may, we'll probably always repeat.

Workplace gluttony doesn't have to fall into that pattern. Let's take some time to reduce it now. Be excellent in your work and own the mindset of quality and a job-well-done over taking on too much for the wrong reasons. It's the ultimate cure for the deadly sin of gluttony.

Deadly Sin #4: Lust

Pope Gregory defined lust as an inordinate craving for the pleasures of the body. At first glance, this seems rather out of touch with the workplace issues I write about, but it's really not.

Lust finds its way into modern work society in two ways. One of course is the obvious: sexual harassment. No doubt you've been subjected to hours of training on how to prevent sexual harassment so I won't spend any time here. You know the two types (quid pro quo and the hostile work environment) have no place whatsoever in our organizations and hopefully any instances you might experience are anomalies which are dealt with swiftly and firmly.

The second, less obvious way we experience lust at work is through ego gratification. It's only speculation on what went through Pope Gregory's mind when he defined lust as a craving for the pleasures of the body so for our purposes, we'll speak of it as something humans strive for that requires continuous increases in order to satisfy.

Lust could, in fact, be our earlier sin of Envy put into action.

What are we talking about?

John is an average employee who is relatively happy at work. Soon he notices that Bill, his co-worker gets a new BMW. Jealousy soon sets in and John finds himself looking in the Sunday paper car ads for a BMW. He buys one, and for a time things are fine. Soon however, he finds himself getting more and more annoyed by Bill's chatter about what he has and what he buys. Armani suits, Rolex watches, Gucci shoes, expensive gifts for his wife, lavish vacations for his family. It goes on and on. Unable to stand it any longer, John gets himself into the one-upmanship game. Soon, John is obsessively attempting to keep pace with Bill. He runs deep into debt. Finally, Bill leaves the company to pursue other opportunities. John's "things" no longer satisfy the need to compete so he keeps up the practice for no other reason than it's just a kind of addiction.

Is this an extreme example? Of course. My point is that the pursuit of material pleasure is a losing game. If the whole purpose of materialism is to compete, or to satisfy a deeper need for acceptance, then it's just a pursuit of pleasure that could in fact be satisfied with something less expensive or dangerous.

What's your point?

Take some time to examine what desires you have. If they're targeted towards a bona fide need, then acquisition of whatever it is you want should satisfy. If not, then look deeper to examine what the real issue is. Is it ego? Competition? Jealously? Probably a good idea to do some exploration to avoid the deadly sin of lust.

Deadly Sin #5: Anger

According to Pope Gregory anger is manifested in the individual who spurns love and opts instead for fury. It is also known as Wrath. If you've ever dealt with angry people at work, you know this is a real issue.

I've spent lots of time talking about angry bosses so we won't dwell there now. I'm more concerned now in dealing with angry co-workers and customers. Anger is an emotional response to outward stimuli. This is a fancy way of saying people get ticked off when actions fail to meet expectations. According to Daniel Goleman, the "guru" of Emotional Intelligence (EI), our brains are open systems, which, unlike our circulatory system that flows in a continuous loop, take in outside information and process it.

What does this mean?

Let's say Sally is a customer service rep in a call center. She's on the line with a customer who is trying to get help with checking e-mail on a new piece of software. The customer is already a little angry after navigating through a seemingly endless phone tree, but because Sally isn't in a great mood herself, the negative vibe she is giving off is entering the open loop of the customer's brain. This intensifies the emotional response to the point where the customer flies into a verbal tirade on the phone and slams the phone down.

Have you ever experienced this?

Did you know the key to diffusing angry people is really quite simple? You simply have to **C.L.A.P.** your way through the process.

C.L.A.P. stands for Clarify, Legitimize, Acknowledge, and Probe. Let's break it down.

C is for clarification. When dealing with angry customers or co-workers, give them some time to vent, then clarify exactly what the issue is. Have them tell the entire story to you and listen actively.

L is for legitimize. Even if you think the customer or co-worker is out of line, you must legitimize their emotion at the very least. Put yourself in their position for a moment to gain perspective. Don't fire back at them even if they've insulted you (or your mother) and don't let your body language communicate your anger.

A is for acknowledge. Again, you don't have to agree with what the customer's problem is, but you must acknowledge it. Don't say "I know how you feel." Instead, try "that sounds very frustrating – I can understand why you might be angry about that _____."

P is for probe. After hearing the entire story, ask the important question, "is that everything or is there something else that's going on here." Your job in the "P" stage is to get every piece of information you need. Only then can you solve the problem in its entirety.

What's your point?

Anger, left unresolved, only grows. The open loop in the brain processes quickly and before you know it, a situation that could have been prevented or at least minimized can grow out of control. Take a moment to collect your thoughts before jumping into a heated situation. You don't have to love all of your co-workers or customers, but you do have a responsibility to treat them with respect and handle anger properly and with maturity.

Deadly Sin #6: Greed

"I did not have 3,000 pairs of shoes, I had 1,060."
Imelda Marcos
(former First Lady of the Philippines)

"I told you I needed to feed my family. They offered me 3 years at $21 million. That's not going to cut it. And I'm not going to sit here and continue to give my children food while this front office takes money out of my pocket. If [owner Glen] Taylor wants to see my family fed, he better cough up some money. Otherwise, you're going to see these kids in one of those Sally Struthers commercials soon."
Latrell Sprewell (former NBA star)

According to Pope Gregory, greed is the desire for material wealth or gain, ignoring the realm of the spiritual. It is also called Avarice or Covetousness. It simply means you want more than your fair share.

Greed in the workplace has obvious results. The media regularly reports examples for all of us to read. This past year, numerous CEOs have been fired for tweaking the finances ensuring their year-end bonuses were maximized. The quotes at the top of this posting are now famous for their absurdity.

How does greed affect us in the workplace? I think in two specific ways.

1. The obvious – embezzling company funds and resources. Taking items that don't belong to you (yes, the ream of paper, pens, and paper clips from the office count too!)

2. Recognition – striving for more than your share of recognition of achievements, often at the expense of other.

You've all seen this before I'm sure. Joe and Sally are co-workers. Sally is the stronger performer, making Joe have to strive harder for recognition. Recognition results in a better appraisal, possible promotion and certainly a year-end bonus. Rather than working harder, he uses political skills, backstabbing, and gossip-spreading to undermine Sally. The desire for recognition goes way beyond performing better. To counter this, Sally soon has to "play the game" which means she can't concentrate on simply doing her job. Work ceases to be fun. Her performance slips. Everybody loses.

The solution?

The definition of greed suggests there is more to life than just striving for material possessions. Take some time to look beyond just getting the next "thing." Quit competing with your co-workers and neighbors and turn the competition within. Grow your SELF and you'll find the other needs won't scream out as being as important. If they're in check, greed automatically shrinks.

Deadly Sin #7: Sloth

According to Pope Gregory, sloth is the avoidance of physical or spiritual work. I guess we all know it better as laziness.

None of us are in a position to judge spiritual sloth, but we've all seen physical sloth in the workplace. There is that one employee who puts in half-effort at everything. If there's a task to be done, they're always the ones who avoid it if they can, or if you engage them, they're only going to do the bare minimum. You might call them slackers, say they have a lack of initiative, or maybe you refer to them as "deadwood."

Slothful people present a risk and money drain for employers in three different ways:

1. They're a drain on resources without adding little, or any value

2. They devote significant company time to devising ways to avoid work at the expense of completing their own job.

3. They increase the workload for their workmates which either causes them to less productive or to simply seek employment elsewhere.

Entire performance management systems are changed or invented to counter the workplace sloth. Documentation of the slothful employee takes a manager out of their most important roles and puts them behind in other important tasks.

What are some strategies to counter sloth?

It's a tough question. After all, sloth begins on the inside. It's an attitude that manifests itself in action (or lack thereof.) There are only a couple of strategies I think will work:

1. Document and confront. This is what most folks resort to. It's time consuming and usually results in limited change.

2. Fire the sloth. Normally, this is the end result of #1. It takes documentation and always presents the risk of the employee filing EEO complaints or taking other action against you.

3. Initiate change from within the sloth. Since sloth is an attitude, it only gets fixed by confronting the issues that result in the slothfulness. Attitudes are just the outward expression of inward values. If this is true, then you'll need to drill down into the source. To do this, you'll need a tool that we'll explore in Chapter 9.

Conclusions

As we think back over these Seven Deadly Workplace Sins, a clear pattern emerges. If we don't first deal with our own assumptions, attitudes and actions, we'll let the Sinners make our life miserable. Let's review what happens when we let difficult people dictate our lives:

1. Difficult people can ground our progress.

If all we do is point fingers at the difficult people around us, we'll lose focus on our own goals and merely seek peace and safety from those around us.

2. Difficult people can paralyze us from growing professionally.

Our focus on handling the difficult folks around us will draw us into the politics and petty games enjoyed by that group. This is a major roadblock in a quest for professional growth.

3. Difficult people can hamper our job security.

Employers quickly lose patience with whiners and troublemakers. Get yourself slinging mud with difficult people and you'll find yourself riding out of the organization on the same bus!

4. Difficult people keep us from dealing with our own "baggage."

By focusing solely on the difficult people, we'll feel by default that we're ok. Here's a newsflash: All of us need work! Quit worrying about fixing the difficult people and look inside first.

About Malcolm O. Munro:

Malcolm O. Munro is the President of **Total Career Mastery, LLC.** He is a nationally-recognized author, speaker, consultant and coach who works with companies and organizations in all industries nationally and internationally.

You can reach him and his associates at:

www.TotalCareerMastery.com

Chapter 8

Employee Engagement and Motivation

By

Jeffrey Salters

A workshop participant, let's call him Dave, asked for advice on turning around his organization. Dave is a senior executive at a hospital. Profits are low. So are productivity, morale and patient service ratings. The only key performance indicator (KPI) constantly rising is employee turnover. In an era where good nurses are in high demand, the hospital has a nurse turnover rate close to 20 percent. They tried the usual tactics – a new strategy, technology, reorganizing. They even brought in new, no-nonsense leadership. Nothing worked. In fact, it got worse. Dave talked about how poorly the nurses regarded the hospital in exit interviews. Condescending doctors and bullying bosses were the norm. When asked how he like working for the hospital, Dave said: "I'd rather not!" So what to do next? The advice: Before you waste more time, effort and money, consider building a better place for people to work.

The research is clear: Happy employees outperform unhappy employees. Better workplaces produce happier, more engaged and more motivated employees. They inspire productivity, creativity, and teamwork, which produce superior business results. According to the research:

- Highly engaged employees were 87 percent less likely to leave their companies than there disengaged counter parts.

- Engaged employees take over 50 percent less sick leave.

- Companies in the top quartile of engagement had 12 percent higher profitability as compared to companies in the bottom quartile.

- Companies with high employee engagement scores had twice the customer loyalty of companies with average ratings.

The disciplines that combine to produce these results include employee engagement, emotional intelligence, positive organizational scholarship, organization development, and others. It would take an entire book to cover each of these topics. Instead, this chapter will introduce the key approaches these disciplines suggest.

The Role of Emotions at Work

When we feel threatened – like when stalked by the proverbial saber tooth tiger – we go into fight-flight-freeze mode. Our prefrontal cortex largely shuts down, which means we fail to think clearly, narrowing our choices, and increasing our chance at survival. In the workplace, the fight-flight-freeze response initiates in response to perceived, non-physical threats. When managers berate employees, for example, their ability to think clearly is compromised, resulting in lower productivity, creativity and overall effectiveness.

Barbara Fredrickson, a preeminent researcher on emotions, speculated that since negative emotions narrow choices to help us survive, then positive emotions must also play an important role. She found that positive emotions – like joy, hope, and pride – broaden our choices, resulting in greater creativity, productivity and teamwork. Managers that seek enhanced employee performance should strive to increase positive emotions at work.

To create better workplaces and happier employees, organizations must help employees:

Work in a Caring Environment

The common denominator of employee engagement and motivation is that employees respond to managers, coworkers and organizations that care about them. Show employees you care and their performance will exceed your expectations. A caring environment creates esprit de corps. It enables the social glue that makes employees feel like they belong to a family. This feeling creates trust, and encourages sharing information, collaboration, and teamwork. These are ingredients for well-functioning organizations.

Your job as a manager is to find ways to show you care that make sense for you and your organization. The rest of this chapter will identify specific approaches managers can take to show employees how much they care.

Find Meaning

Employees that believe their work contributes to a greater good, feel compelled to work harder. We like to believe the products and services we deliver make the world a better place. Eighty-three percent of employees say it's very important that their lives have meaning. Organizations can help employees find meaning in their lives through work. When organizational values align with employee values, employees tend to believe in the mission of the organization. Companies whose employees feel their work fills a larger purpose have 5 to 15 percent higher profitability, and 30 to 50 percent lower turnover. The reason: Purpose inspires dedication, creativity, and production.

Unfortunately most organizations do a poor job identifying how employees' work ties to organizational mission or how the mission fills a societal purpose. So how can managers help employees find meaning in their work?

- Regularly communicate organizational vision, mission and values. Make it clear to employees who they serve and how customers benefit from your products and services. Describe the crucial role products and services play in the lives of your customers, and on society.

- Consistently live your values. Employees trust and believe in organizations that "walk the talk." Nothing creates cynicism quicker than organizations that act contrary to their stated values.

- Help each employee connect work to the mission. Not all employees make products or deliver services that directly impact customers. If employees work in administrative areas, for example, let them know how their work supports the primary producers of products and services.

- Ask employees what they value about their work. Researchers are sometimes surprised by the many ways employees find meaning in their work. If managers can identify what employees find meaningful, they can help them attain that meaning consistently.

Pursue Interesting Work

People work harder at jobs they enjoy. We sometimes quibble over terms like love, passion, and bliss. Here's the bottom line: We like work that is its own reward. We will engage in work that feels like a hobby, that we'd do for free. We will do it until we become good at it. We'll invest time and effort to become better. This investment leads to superior results.

Those who reach the highest levels in their professions talk about the irresistible urge that compelled them to practice their calling. Bill Gates, as a teenager, learned to become an expert at computer programming because: "It was my obsession. I skipped athletics. I went up there [the computer center at the University of Washington] at night. We were programming on weekends. It would be a rare week that we wouldn't get 20 or 30 hours in."

When engrossed in work they enjoy, people enter a state Mihalyi Csikszentmihalyi calls flow. It's where you lose the sense of time and place and lose yourself in the activity. Those who experience flow report feeling tremendous enjoyment. They look forward to working because, although it may take a great deal of time and effort, it never really feels like work. Compare this attitude with employees that show up just to collect a paycheck. Which employee do you think will be more motivated and productive?

Managers can help employees pursue interesting work by:

- Screening and hiring based on the match between their interests and the company's opportunities. This is difficult, because employees can often convince interviewers of their passion for work, only to prove unsatisfied later. Companies can improve their odds by using behavioral interviews and screening programs.

- Job Crafting – enabling employees to redesign and shape their work so that it is more personally satisfying, and fits their skills and interests.

- Using employee strengths. Employees that use their strengths – skills and abilities at which they excel – on a daily basis are far more satisfied with work than those who rarely use their strengths.

Develop Skills

Maslow taught us that people universally seek self-actualization. He defined it as: "...man's desire for fulfillment...the tendency to become actually what he is potentially: to become everything that one is capable of becoming..." When employees love what they do, they want to do it at higher levels – seeking skill development to fulfill their potential. Companies need highly skilled employees to deliver superior products and services to customers. This is a win-win formula. When employees develop advanced skills, they need workplace challenges to avoid boredom, and to ensure flow states continue – flow happens when skills match work challenges. Therefore, the greater the skills, the more complex the work challenges employees are able to solve.

Managers who want to help employees develop their skills should:

- Coach employees to create development plans that identify the knowledge, skills and abilities they will need to meet future business challenges.

- Identify ways employees can gain new skills – through training, coaching mentoring, rotations, etc.

- Allow employees to attend conferences, or join associations, or other professional organizations that can help them develop their skills.

Provide Feedback

Employees complain they don't always know whether they're doing their jobs well, or how to improve. To be their best, employees need feedback. There are two types of feedback: positive and constructive. Each is described below.

Positive Feedback

Employees need to feel valued. They require praise and recognition for a job well done. Without feedback, employees feel disrespected and unappreciated. Feeling "dissed," employees fail to perform and eventually leave the organization.

Praise releases dopamine in the brain, which employees experience as pleasurable. Employees who get positive feedback crave more. They will repeat performance or engage in other practices that are likely to elicit feedback. Fredrickson's research says that high-performing teams receive 5.6 times more positive than negative comments. Low-performing teams receive 2.8 negative comments for every positive. This doesn't mean that managers must count individual or organizational positive-to-negative comment ratio, but they should be aware of the need to provide substantially more positive comments than they're probably accustomed to.

During workshops, when asked why they don't offer more positive feedback, managers' most frequent responses include: "Why should I give positive feedback when they're just doing their jobs?" or "I work hard without praise. Why aren't they self-motivated?" These attitudes, while understandable, don't change the fact that employees desire feedback and will respond with better performance.

In addition to offering regular positive feedback, managers should offer specific feedback. Too often managers simply say: "Good job." It's more effective if managers tell employees exactly what they did well: "I like how you stayed calm when that customer lost his temper. You did a great job remaining professional under difficult circumstances." That way, employees know what behavior to repeat.

Constructive Feedback

Constructive feedback provides potentially the most challenging conversations managers and employees will have. Not surprisingly, managers offer it even less frequently than positive feedback. The main reason most managers cite is the potential for emotional confrontation. Because conflict is scary, managers avoid it. However, without constructive feedback employees miss a vital ingredient in their professional development. They fail to improve and organizations suffer. The key to delivering constructive feedback effectively is to use language that reduces the chances of emotional upset. Here are the principles:

- Describe employee behavior objectively, free of judgment. Avoid labels that demean employees like "lazy" or "stupid." Stick to facts.

- Describe the behavior's impact on you, coworkers, or customers – "When you speak to employees that way, they get offended..."

- Discuss the employee's perspective. Let them explain their position regarding the issue. Expect to have a discussion. Be sure to listen actively.

- Describe the preferred employee behavior.

- Reach agreement on future behavior, expectations and if necessary, consequences.

Involve Employees in Important Decisions

In most organizations major change happens from the top down. Senior leaders tend to naturally be change agents. And since they usually orchestrate the change, they are prepared. In lower levels of the organization change is frightening. What passes for change management in most organizations is making a compelling case for change, and creating and communicating the vision. Employees report feeling frustrated that no one consulted them on the impact change has on their jobs. They complain, not just about having to learn new software or technology for example, but that their jobs are now harder and that the new systems don't actually improve operations. The reasons could be simple "resistance to change," or it could be that the solution really doesn't perform as advertised.

Employees, unable to have any say in operations that impact the way they work or experience the organization, feel like they're working for an uncaring bureaucracy or that they are unimportant. When the organization shows it doesn't care about employees, employees will return the favor.

An organization development maxim states: "People tend to support what they help to create." Employees don't reject their own ideas. The need for a major change may come from the top, however the implementation needs to consider how it will affect anyone who uses it or is substantially impacted by it. Employees will buy into processes and systems they're allowed to shape. Their ideas may also deliver value, because lower-level employees are often closer to the customer or process. This approach may take more time upfront, but it saves time and money in the long run.

Conclusion

Business trends come and go. Senior leaders pursue the latest business fads to keep up with the "corporate Joneses." But the principles that create engaged employees aren't fleeting. Treating employees like you care will always deliver results. If you say you care in your corporate communications, your actions must prove it. Resist the temptation to make this solely Human Resources' responsibility. Employee engagement and motivation are everyone's job. Senior leaders set the tone at the top and it cascades throughout the organization. For all future practices, think about the emotional and psychological impact they are likely to have. Show you care and employees will perform.

About Jeffery Salters:

Jeff Salters is an experienced consultant and trainer with expertise in building engaged work cultures in the public and private sector. He can be reached at:

www.EngagingWorkplaces.com

References

Fredrickson, B.L., Mancuso, R.A., Branigan, C., & Tugade, M.M. (2000). The Undoing Effects of Positive Emotions. *Motivation and Emotion, 24,* 237-258.

Gladwell, M. (2008). *Outliers: The Story of Success.* New York: Little, Brown and Company.

Kruse, K. (2012). Why Employee Engagement? *Forbes.* Document available at *http://www.forbes.com/sites/kevinkruse/2012/09/04/why-employee-engagement/.* Accessed April 18, 2013.

Pink, D.H. (2009). *Drive: The Surprising Truth About What Motivates Us.* New York: Riverhead Books.

Wagner, R., Harter, J.K. (2006). *12: The Elements of Great Managing.* New York: Gallup Press

Chapter 9

Establishing a LEAN Culture
By
Tom Strickler

I want to start by saying thank you for taking the time to read this book! There is no doubt plenty of essential information everyone of us will be able to put to immediate use. While some of the other chapters concentrate on the "people" portion of the equation here we will exam the work that gets done by looking at it from the process level. As an emerging business leader hopefully you have heard a lot of buzz about LEAN methodologies or at least that they can produce more profits for an organization. While they can certainly streamline processes, which saves time and money, they also have a much more profound impact. Sadly, this benefit is one that many managers seem to overlook. What is this amazing byproduct that must not be ignored you ask? Simple, the ability for them to instill pride, satisfaction and loyalty in a workforce!

Before we go any further we should take a moment to cover some basics of LEAN. While we touch on these ask yourself how you could implement these tools in your organization.   Once you have this target in mind it will be easier to relate to your current role as we discuss implementation and sustainment steps.

LEAN and Six Sigma are two Continuous Process Improvement (CPI) practices most often referenced in business.   One common mistake is for these to be either thought of as interchangeable or combined approaches. Remember LEAN is about process or removing "what is not needed" while Six Sigma is about product quality or "what is wrong" and needs to be fixed.   LEAN identifies what is non-value added, and saves money through practices that result in the identification and removal of waste.   Six Sigma helps us to improve with the identification and removal of defects.   While the goal here is to help you successfully introduce LEAN these steps could also be effective should your goal be Six Sigma programs.

In the battle of "Good vs. Evil" we can always count on our hero LEAN to defeat the gang of criminal masterminds that lurk in every form of business.   I decided that just because this subject is about doing work that doesn't mean we can't have fun with it.   This is why I have created a story as a backdrop for the tools you can use in your career.   We will imagine Waste as a diabolical band of outlaws, one that will rob you of your profits. There are eight typical forms of waste we look for using LEAN, for our purposes our bandits will be:

- ➢ Non-Value Added Processing
- ➢ Defects
- ➢ Over Production
- ➢ Waiting
- ➢ Transportation
- ➢ Inventory (Too Much or Too Little)
- ➢ Motion

Never fear, our "Sheriff" has a keen eye for problems and he won't hesitate to call on Marshal LEAN and his Deputies to help save the day. These Deputies that will be dispatched to save the day are:

- ➢ Root Cause Analysis (RCA)
- ➢ Value Stream Mapping (VSM)
- ➢ Theory of Constraints (TOC)
- ➢ 5S or 5S+1
- ➢ Business Process Reengineering (BPR)
- ➢ Voice of the Customer (VOC)

As we go through this story I will pause to offer you observations that will help you transfer the events to your individual situations. These will be identified by a Sheriff's badge that looks like this:

It may be helpful for you to keep notes and write down any similarities that you may be able to leverage for immediate results. Hope you're ready because we need to get a move on!

So, saddle up partners and let's ride!

TROUBLE IN THE TOWN OF PROFITS

The tumbleweed rolled down the middle of Main Street in the Town of Profits surrounded by a huge cloud of dust. The sun was rising slowly and the light was painting the backdrop of this bustling boomtown. People happily went about their business unaware that hard times had just arrived. Sure there was word of a band of outlaws in these parts but that kind of trouble wouldn't happen to them. Little did they know their luck had just run out and they too would fall victim to the Gang of the Eight Deadly Wastes.

As they reached the edge of town the despicable leader "Ned Non-Value-added Processing" raised his hand to stop the others. He quickly surveyed the scene and turned to bark orders that would dispatch the others to take their toll. His henchmen, which included "Willie Waiting, Timmy Transportation, Ollie Over Production, Ivan Inventory, Ulysses Under Utilizing People, Drew Defects, and Moses Motion all sat waiting for him.

He first set eyes on Suzanne's Saloon where he knew a thirsty cow hand would despise what his man Willie Waiting could do. Willie walked in and immediately persuaded the barkeep that from now on there would be a two hour wait for every drink ordered by making them think it would make them spend more from being there longer. Business came to a screeching halt as card games lost players, and music faded leaving the place empty except for the employees and an old red bone hound.

Next he sent Timmy Transportation to go check in on Bucks Bank. Buck showed them a new way of sorting and handling the money that would require each teller to pick up and move each stack at least ten times. They would have to count them each time so it would of course be more secure by making them more accountable. Every time they stopped helping customers to move and count the bills Timmy would just smile and spin his spurs on the old wood floor boards.

Ollie Over Production had a specialty in each town that he couldn't wait to get started on. He made his way over to Billy the Blacksmith to explain how the hot job could be done so much easier. You see he told Billy, if he would just go ahead and pound out four extra shoes for every horse sooner or later he would only have to shape them half the time he put them on. Billy liked the sound of that and could already see himself over at Suzanne's having a cold drink in the middle of the day!

Then there was Ivan Inventory, one of the sneakiest snakes in the whole bunch. Ivan strolled into Ginger's General Store and slowly browsed around. When he was asked if he needed help he began asking for everything on the shelves in different colors, sizes, or flavors. Ginger was frustrated it seemed none of the old stand byes were going suit him and she would not be able to help him at all. Ivan waited until she was most upset then started giving her his perfected sales pitch. She needed to expand the quantities and options she had on hand. No more time for the old order and wait method for her customers as the times were changing and she needed change with them. Ginger ran to her order books and started making out lists of what would be nice to have around.

Ulysses Under Utilizing People liked to find a different service provider to target in each town and his boss made him happy with that day's choice. Ben's had recently installed a second chair in his barbershop and with Ben's son Bucyrus alongside him customers rarely had to wait. Ulysses knew if he could persuade Ben that if he had the boy stand out front with a sandwich board containing weather updates people would come to read them and stay for haircuts. Later on that day Bucyrus found himself standing in the hot afternoon sun with a sign that read "Hot and Sunny" as the flies swarmed around his head.

Meanwhile Drew Defects stopped by Sam's Suits and offered to show him how he could make up to eight times the amount of suits by skipping a few steps like measuring the cloth and using patterns every time. Pretty soon old Sam was hanging up suits quicker than a roadrunner riding a sunbeam! He could already see himself standing in line over at that slow bank he visited earlier that very morning with huge stacks of bills to be deposited.

Finally the very menacing Moses Motion made his way into Hank's Hotel to check into the many ways he could cause them to fail. It didn't take long to get them to move all of the room keys up to each individual room so they wouldn't get mixed up at the counter. No worries if someone had to wait while the desk clerk ran to each floor and made a check to see what rooms were empty. It wasn't long before Hank had to hire four or five extra employees and it was all he could do just to keep track of who was where doing what.

This madness carried on for well over a month before the Sheriff made it back to town from his lawman convention in Capital City. He knew something was amiss right away due to the long lines, upset consumers and poor old Bucyrus standing out there in the street with that dumb sign that said "Hot and Cloudy" which anyone passing by could easily anyway. He investigated by making his rounds to check in on what the ruckus was about. He couldn't make heads or tails out of it and each stop he made left him more puzzled than he had ever been. He stood looking around at the mess things had become for what seemed like an eternity before he spied the eight strange horses tied up over at Billy's. He knew right away what was wrong and shuffled back to his office to find the flyer he had picked up at the convention. There was a special group of lawmen trained in this exact type of wrong doing that was destroying Profits for everyone that lived there. He could still save them but he had to ask fast! He grabbed the paper tight in his hand and rode out of town on his faithful horse Josey as the Sun set slowly behind bringing the darkness.

He rode all night and early into the next day stopping only to eat a piece of deer jerky and feed Josey a corn muffin. He made it back to Capital City just before Sunrise and found his way to the office of Marshal LEAN. Marshal LEAN assembled his team of Deputies JIT, VOC, BPR, 5S+1, TOC, VSM, and RCA. They listened to what the Sheriff had to say and they made a plan for who would stop which bandit before any more damage was done.

As the officers rode back into Profits it looked more like a ghost town than the commerce hub it had recently been. Suzanne's had a steady flow of people going in but they would only stay for about 15 or 20 minutes then come right back out again. That was strange as many of those folks; especially the regulars would usually spend hours at a time there. Marshal LEAN Sent his expert Deputy VOC (Voice of the Customer) to investigate the problem. Deputy VOC sat down with everyone that worked there and proceeded to ask a series of questions designed to help them see why the customer is the most important person in any business. It didn't take long before the old way of serving the customers was reinstated and Deputy VOC was walking out the door with the pesky criminal "Willie Waiting" in custody.

★ *This would seem like common sense to most but it is easy to lose track of a customer focus when we are looking for the best business plan. In fact we can see it almost every single day without even looking that hard. It could be* *at a restaurant where making a substitution isn't allowed because someone decided it was too hard to get the order right or know what to charge. In the customers eyes all they see is you have the means to make this request happen but not the desire. Just today I went to my bank to request a new ATM/Debit card because mine would no longer work. The expiration date on the card would be in two months anyway so that should be an easy thing to do. You can imagine how frustrated I was when they told me in order to order a new card early they would have to charge me $10.00! I couldn't believe that they would rather risk losing me as a customer altogether than just order a new card six weeks early. They did offer to replace the card for only $4.95 if that would make it more acceptable. They were missing the point of the whole situation it had nothing to do with the money. After thirty minutes of debate and a call by them to their Main Branch I was able to get the cards taken care of as they always should have been. Sadly, I think the lesson to be learned escaped the tellers as a whole. Truly great organizations will always strive to go that extra mile. Simply put, they find a way to say "yes" instead of "no" whenever it is feasible.*

Deputy 5S+1 (Sort, Sstraighten, Shine, Standardize, Sustain and Safety) was dispatched to the bank to lend a hand. Once he took one look at the mess the place had become he got right to work in helping the nice folks there run through the 5S+1 organization method. Having everything all worked out and running smooth again put a smile on everyone's face, most of all the customers! Deputy 5S+1 put the cuffs on "Timmy Transportation" and led him out the door.

★ *It might help you to think of 5S+1 as a way to improve your business if you consider it as a Spring Cleaning meets Diet and Exercise routine that you can't quit for any reason. The first three Sort, Straighten and Shine are the cleaning and organizing half while Standardize, Sustain and Safety are more of a moving forward with a plan much like committing to diet and exercise. Once you have taken the important step to do the first half don't let the problems back in by getting lazy and eating a whole bag of cookies. Stick to your guns and make the better process the new normal!*

Deputy JIT (Just in Time) sprinted over to the Billy's to see why there were horseshoes piling up everywhere. Billy was tricked into believing that having the work done before the customer needed it would make future service faster. What he didn't consider was that all that time spent doing work that had no current need put him farther and farther behind for the customers he needed to help today. He started adding up the cost of making and storing all those shoes and couldn't believe he was so easy to fool. Ollie had made many business professionals go down that same path, he was good at what he did. The good thing was that thanks to the work of Deputy JIT those days were over and he waved goodbye as Ollie Overproduction was taken away with his head hung down in shame.

★ *While this is primarily a situation that would be found in a traditional manufacturing environment it can happen in just about any type of business. Be sure and keep your eyes and ears open for any sign of anticipating demand by working ahead. If you hear any talk of completing work that has not been identified by a need be sure and ask the "what if" question. You know the one; "what if we build these, or do this work and then nobody asks for it?" Who's going to pay for it? Don't let it be you!*

Over at Ginger's General Store things had gotten way out of hand. She had piles and piles of merchandise everywhere and there wasn't even room to walk the aisles. Deputy BPR (Business Process Reengineering) jumped right in and started digging her out of the mess that was made. He was able to show her how the various methods of reducing inventory while increasing throughput by advertising in store specials and synchronizing her supply chain processes would fix the problem. Lucky for her she was able to return a majority of the unneeded over stock and make room for her customers to shop. Deputy BPR arrested Izekel Inventory and wasted no time hauling him off to jail.

★ *One of the best sources for anyone to use when it comes to BPR implementation is benchmarking. What is working for others is always better than trying to reinvent the wheel. Don't forget to look outside of your business area as many of the greatest ideas are universally advantageous to apply. If you are managing a rental car firm maybe that sandwich place across town has a key to help you too. There is no way to put a value on the potential networking can bring. Find a way to get involved in professional organizations or local commerce groups and make new friends. Offer as much help as you can and don't forget to listen to what others are saying. A wise colleague of mine one time named Jerry Lawler (not the wrestler) had a saying that sums this up. He would say; "Two heads are always better than one as long as one of them is mine!" I thought he was pretty egotistical when I first heard that but luckily I asked him to explain. He said that if he wasn't in the conversation he would have no chance of learning something new. That is why it is always better for one to be his...or yours for that matter.*

Ulysses Under Utilizing People had pretty much destroyed things between Bucyrus and his pa Ben over at the barber shop. Bucyrus couldn't help but feel like he was wasting his time there and he was dragging the stupid weather sign behind as he made his way in to quit on the spot. Luckily Deputy TOC (Theory of Constraints) showed up just in time to identify the problem. He explained that by moving Bucyrus out into the street may have generated more business but not enough to account for what was lost by the bottleneck of having only one barber chair open. Not to mention, you don't want the high cost of trying to replace a valuable employee whose frustration had pushed them to leave the company. Pretty soon Ben and Bucyrus were laughing and joking again side by side as they cut and shaved all the hair that had gotten unruly for their loyal customers. Deputy TOC took great pride in removing Ulysses from the building and reuniting him with the rest of the gang who had already arrived at the town jail.

★ *While the example here is very extreme when it comes to creating a bottleneck or process constraint be warned that they are seldom that easy to identify. They can be the smallest piece of what we do but cause so many problems. If you have any step that seems to be waiting on the one before it you need to immediately figure out why that is.*

The other side of this being that by Ben ignoring what his son could do for the business he almost lost some much needed talent. Another much more subtle way in which we can ignore talent is by not taking the time to listen to an idea. You never know who will be the one to figure out the next big thing but starting with the people who are doing the activities every day is always a great place to start!

The problems caused by Drew Defects over at Sam's had created a massive amount of damage. Deputy VSM (Value Stream Mapping) knew he was exactly the right man for the job when he walked in and witnessed the huge mess. He quickly grasped Sam and started outlining the process of suit making one step at a time. Sam was eager to understand the problem so he was very helpful at explaining each and every detail so they could document what was being done. Once they had it all mapped out the deputy explained that value could only be found in the steps a customer would be willing to pay for. If there was something being done that didn't help the cloth become clothes then it needed to be eliminated. As the most efficient process of making a suit became clear the unneeded and inappropriate steps that were causing the defects were eliminated. Drew Defects was cuffed and taken away so Sam could clean up the mess and get things running smooth again.

★ *I cannot stress enough the importance of learning how VSM can be applied and administered for managers at all levels. Being able to conduct a mapping event doesn't mean that a huge investment in time and resources must be allocated. One of these incredible events can often be run in as little as half a day with an infinite return on investment. If you haven't already done so you need to do some research on this technique and start thinking about how you can use it in your business?*

Deputy RCA (Root Cause Analysis) went over to Hank's Hotel and called all of the employees into a meeting right away. Once he had everyone in one place he started by asking them "Why are you keeping the keys in the doors?" The answer was that it makes things easier at the front desk without them being in the way. Next he asked; "Why were they in the way?" A desk worker said because they were behind the counter. "Why were they behind the counter?" So we could issue them to the guests at check in. "Why then are you keeping them in the doors of the empty rooms?" All at once they pointed at Moses Motion who was trying to hide behind the front drapes and said because he had told them it was a great idea. Right away a big group of them jumped up and ran up the stairs and down the hall grabbing all the keys that weren't being used. Meanwhile another group had grabbed ahold of

Moses as he tried to make his escape and handed him over to the deputy. They all shook hands with Deputy RCA and thanked him for all his help. Just before Moses was led out of the building a little red haired boy rain up and kicked him right in the shin which caused him to howl out in pain. The boy's Grandma leaned back in her chair and said "Serves you right" then spit a big stream of tobacco juice into a nearby spittoon.

★ *Root Cause Analysis is one of the most versatile tools and anyone can do it. Often referred to as the "Five Whys" because all the process consists of is repeatedly asking why until the problem is easily identified. It may not take five times to figure out the problem, and it may take a whole lot more so don't make the mistake of stopping too soon. While you may find a process issue it may not be the problem you are looking for. If you can't answer the question with a justifiable response keep going until you can.*

Back at the jail house all of the deputies were celebrating their recent work as the Sheriff shook hands with the Marshal Lean on the front porch. They all turned to look when they heard a horse approaching from across town. The man rode up and stopped right in front of the jail, removed his hat and offered them a pleasant greeting. The Marshal raised his hand to the others and stepped down onto the dirt street so he could speak with the man.

He asked him what his business was in town and if they might be of service to him in any way. The man began to explain that it seemed like a group of his boys had gotten into some trouble by causing mischief and wanted to know if he could have them released to him so they could be on their way. It was the conversation that the Marshal hated to have. There was nothing within his powers that he could use to keep the gang detained and he knew he would have to let them go only to repeat the process in another time and another place. The deputies knew that the time to celebrate was over and they needed to be ready to act when the next call came in. Experience had taught them to never let their guard down when it comes to the battle with waste!

It is on that note we leave the efficient little town of Profits and remind everyone this story could have happened anywhere. Stay vigilant against these villains always ready to make sure waste knows it isn't wanted. If it does find a way into your business don't hesitate to call on Marshal LEAN and his Deputies to help you set things back in order.

There are as many schools of thought on which approach is the best and when to use which tools as there are LEAN practitioners. The best thing I can say is make sure you have a certified LEAN professional on your team. Many larger organizations have added these experts to the staff however it is more common for them to be outsourced from a consulting firm on an as needed basis.

So, you have identified a need and coordinated with a LEAN facilitator to build your strategy for success, now what?

When organizational leadership fully commits to adopting a LEAN vision they must follow-up by showing their unwavering support for all initiatives. Only by truly doing this can the potential be unlimited. There is one common mistake that I have seen many seasoned managers make, they fail to keep the momentum once they have gained it. For you football fans, think of your team getting a turnover that puts them in scoring position only to make the mistake of turning the ball back over with a fumble on the first play from scrimmage. They were given the opportunity to score but let it slip away, and you now you are upset and disgusted. You may even find yourself pointing a finger at the guy who dropped the ball and saying a few things that are not very nice. Nobody wants to be that guy that drops the ball. In fact I guarantee nobody is madder than he is about not protecting the ball. Sadly, many business leaders do just that when they are given the "LEAN Ball" in scoring position, they drop it. They start off as the new running phenom of the league and pile up the scores by recognizing and rewarding those employees that are the early adapters. The lucky ones who were part of the first two or three projects are showered with attention. Than the excitement begins to taper off, and suddenly just falls off the cliff all at once. This is where the fumble happens and is often only a few short months later. These incredible changes are still resulting in remarkable results but they are viewed by everyone as having less importance in the eyes of those who really matter. Not soon after that happens you can bet the employees, or the "Process Owners" begin to feel participating isn't as important anymore because nobody cares. Let's take a timeout here for a second. I want to take a moment to touch on what I just said here, specifically calling them "Process Owners" and mentioning how they feel. Listen up; it doesn't matter if you call yourself a Manager, a Leader, a Supervisor or whatever you need to know remember this. If you don't have your finger on the pulse of what matters to your team you are missing out on at least 80% of their amazing potential. These environments will produce an extremely disengaged workforce and cause retention problems, discipline actions and safety incidents to skyrocket. Listen to your workforce, respect the information that the people doing the tasks are telling you. Always strive to provide them with pride in ownership and you will be their favorite lawman!

About Tom Strickler:

Tom Strickler is currently president of Value Added Results, LLC located in Southeastern Wisconsin. Specializing in Business Performance Evaluations and Strategic Improvement Planning, Tom has worked with many corporations and government agencies in developing innovative new processes to boost efficiencies. Tom has a unique three pillared approach from his extensive experience in the areas of business and professional counseling. Process Improvement is conducted as a Certified LEAN/Six Sigma Practitioner/Green Belt and graduate of various advanced courses through the Lean Enterprise Institute. A Workforce Education & Development Major at Southern Illinois University, Tom has developed many training programs ranging from Human Resources topics to specific Technical Training programs. Combined with his research and authoring of unique methodologies for Management & Leadership honed through 20+ years of active duty military service and corporate consulting assignments Tom will provide aspiring professionals and forward thinking organizations a well-balanced systemic overview to find their optimal performance capabilities! To contact Tom for more services and information please email at: **tom@valueaddedresults.com** or phone (262) 473-9309, or find him on the web at **ValueAddedResults.com.**

Chapter 10

Surround Yourself with Great People, and Then Take Care of Them
By

Denise F. Williams

Behind every good manager, there is a good team. Behind every great manager, there is a great team the manager carefully assembled, developed, and cultivated. If you surveyed accomplished managers about their success, few could honestly claim they achieved their success by themselves. They had a team of people, large or small, vast or intimate, who ventured on a two-way journey with them. By two-way journey, there was give and take between the manager and the team. While the team members gave of themselves in supporting the manager and the organizational goals, the manager reciprocated by supporting the team members. One way or another, the manager ensured the team members exceled and performed up to their fullest potential, and the employees took pride in their performance. That is what successful management is all about. In short, effective managers surround themselves with great people and then take care of them.

SURROUND YOURSELF WITH GREAT PEOPLE

Consider how to surround yourself with quality people by using the Five-W approach: *Who, What, When, Where,* and *Why.* To begin, *Who* do you chose to surround you, and *What* characteristics do they have? The type of person you are seeking for your team is a true team player. Incredibly, there are people who simply do not know how to work as a part of a team. Team work means putting team and task before oneself, and often there are egos that cannot adapt to such a concept. If a single ego or self-serving attitude interrupts the team, progress can be slowed or brought to a halt. In some cases, team work may mean assigning specific tasks to individual members, who are then expected to stay in their lanes. Again, ego may cause lane jumping and thus, a ceasing of productivity. Selecting true team players is a key step and will have a positive impact on future success.

Team work also depends on respect and trust among the team members. If a team member violates a basic premise of the team's norms, respect and trust are gone, and team efforts begin to erode. Your team members must be able to respect and trust each other, and likewise, you need to be able to respect and trust them. These are two characteristics that should be of great importance to you. In saying that, you also want to seek team members who are loyal – loyal to the team, loyal to the organization, loyal to the goals and objectives of the organization, and loyal to you. Loyalty is a matter of believing in and dedicating oneself to someone or to something else. A loyal team member will perform assigned tasks due to loyalties to teammates and a belief in attaining the goal. If loyalties are elsewhere, it will be difficult at best for the member to contribute fully to attaining the goal.

Good judgment and fortitude are similarly strong characteristics to pursue in your team members. Regardless of the level of management at which you operate, your subordinate team members will be called upon to make decisions. You need to be able to trust their judgment in making those decisions. You also need to trust that they will have the fortitude to give you honest feedback based on their sound judgment. If you want a team of people who tell you only what you want to hear and who always agree with you, then you have missed the concept of team. Successful managers do not want yes-zombies working for them. They want a good mix of ideas; they need to be presented all the facts; and, they need to be able to trust the judgment of their subordinates. You need team members with the sound judgment and solid fortitude to tell you when you are wrong.

You must seek intelligent people to surround you. They need to be proficient in their areas of concentration. "Area of expertise" must be just that – expertise. It does you little good if you are counting on an accountant who cannot count. You may not be able to be the intellectual genius in all the areas that are important to you, but you must have people who are. In fact, the probability is you do not know everything about everything. If you do, why are you not ruling the world? Thus, the logic flow would submit that since you are not ruling the world, you need people around you who are intelligent in their areas. You have to be able to trust their intellect and expertise. Seek intelligent life forms. Never be afraid to learn something from your subordinates!

This list of characteristics could continue endlessly, but the final two key traits to be considered here are drive and motivation. Driven people are assets to anything they pursue. Provided the drive is positive, having them in your organization can only result in positive outcomes. In the same respect, motivation is often very contagious within a team or an organization. Finding a driven, motivated player is like hiring your own full time inspirational speaker. Your speaker will motivate and inspire other team members, which will automatically lead to more productivity.

Now that you know *Who* you are looking for and *What* characteristics they must have, *When* do you look for them? The simple answer is constantly. You should always pursue that next great team player. Do you think professional football teams quit scouting because it is the off season? Or because they have a full team? Or even because they just won the Super Bowl? No, they are constantly looking for that next big thing, and they will make room for it when they find it. When you are constantly looking for the right people, you may find them to fill the right positions, you may not have the position open. That is all right. You can either position the people elsewhere in a place you might still be able to utilize their expertise, keep them in mind for the future, or make a recommendation to a colleague. That colleague may do the same for you in the future. Never stop looking for your next great quarterback.

Now, *Where* do you consider placing the people you find? You need to actively search for team members at least two levels down from you. These are positions with which you should be familiar enough to directly influence. These have more direct access to you and therefore can provide you with sound feedback from their perspective, as well as that of their subordinates. Ideally, surrounding yourself with great people at all levels is the proactive way to ensure success in your organization. Great managers build great teams of great people below them, who build teams of great people below them, and so on. However, for your team members one level down, it is critical to employ team players who you respect and trust; who are intelligent, driven, and motivated; who have good judgment and fortitude; and, who are particularly loyal to you. Additionally, you may find yourself with an inner circle of team members who are your most trusted advisors. These may be by position, but are more likely in your inner circle because of a special trust and confidence you have in them. It may be a few or just one, but this is where you place only the best. Surrounding yourself with great people is particularly important for your inner circle. Loyalty, judgment, and fortitude are never more crucial.

Lastly, *Why* is it necessary to be so precise in choosing your team of great people? All too many managers think they can do it all by themselves. The fact is they cannot, and neither can you. A strong, productive organization is the result of a strong, productive team plus strong management. A strong, productive team is comprised of great people. As the manager of this organization, having great people bolsters both the organization and you, and the success of both.

THE CAVEATS

However, there are a few caveats. Employing great people means doing something else with those who are not great. That is correct; it means cutting them loose. It can be uncomfortable, but it is necessary. Getting rid of the mediocrity makes room for greatness. Since you are constantly looking for and finding great people, but not having positions because of mediocre people, then you have a problem. Make room for the greatness you are finding.

Another caveat deals with timing. If you are new to an organization, be careful about bringing in an entirely new team too soon, or letting the old team go too soon. Everyone deserves a first chance before you cut them loose. Bringing in your own team immediately to replace the current team sends a distasteful message. You do not know the quality of the current team. If they were stars and now they are gone, what does that tell everyone else? Give the current team their first chance.

The concluding caveat relates to choices. What if you have little choice about the team with which you have been provided? Or, what if you cannot cut people loose as quickly as you would like? In these cases, you must develop those around you into great team members. Entire books have been written about how to develop the average employee into a great team member. This is not an easy challenge.

HOW TO DEVELOP THE AVERAGE EMPLOYEE

Consider the earlier addressed characteristics: good team player, respect, trust, loyalty, judgment, fortitude, intelligence, drive and motivation. Now, determine how to develop and strengthen these characteristic in your mediocre subordinates. Team work in individuals may be cultivated by establishing a successful working team they will want to join. Watching how others work well together may set a positive example for someone who needs to learn or strengthen team work skills. Start with small teams, and build from there.

Respect and trust may not be simple to develop, but if individuals are aware these are important to you, they will view them as important. No doubt, people must earn the respect and trust of their fellow workers – that goes for the boss as well. If you set the standards high and live up to them, you will gain the respect of your subordinates. There is a good chance they will want to earn your respect in the same way. Equally, earned trust works two ways. In most any relationship, the more trust one puts in another, the more it is reciprocated, and thus the more it continues to grow. Loyalty is another trait that may not be developed but must be earned. Along with respect and trust, this is about establishing the appropriate culture in your organization. If the people around you experience an atmosphere of loyalty, it will become infectious. If they know you have their backs, they are more likely to have yours.

Experience over time and a good gut may contribute to one's ability to make good judgment calls, but the skill can also be learned. While it is natural for those great people around you, do not give up on the others. With time, they can learn to make the right call and provide sound advice. The more experience they get, and the more confidence they build, the easier it becomes for them. Likewise with intelligence, although natural for some, maybe a course or two would bring another individual up to speed. However, it may be the case of a square peg being forced into a round hole, and you need to find the correct hole for the square peg, where intellectual requirement and intellectual capability are the same. Putting the right pegs in the right holes is a tough task, but sometimes that is all it takes to get the wheels turning.

Lastly, how do you develop motivation? As a manager and leader, it is your task regardless to motivate your subordinates. One of the simplest ways to motivate people is to maintain a positive attitude and stay motivated yourself. You may be amazed at how viral a positive, motivated attitude can be, and when the boss is motivated, others will follow suit. If you cannot choose motivated team members, your task is to motivate them yourself. Even if you have a motivated team, your job is to continue to motivate.

NOW TAKE CARE OF THEM

At this point, you have either surrounded yourself with great people or are still in the process of getting those great people on board. Either way, the other major step is to take care of them by venturing onto the two-way street. The list of ways to take care of your subordinates is endless, but an examination of just a few of the two-way streets will provide a good start. The term "two-way" is used to partially answer the question of why. Besides the obvious reason that taking care of your people is the right thing to do, in these two-way examples you will find the quid pro quo effect. That is not to say you give in order to get something in return, but instead this give and take effect produces positive results for the organization, and that is really what this is all about.

An atmosphere of loyalty was addressed earlier, and this is the best example of the two-way street. You need people around you who are loyal, but loyalty-up demands loyalty-down! Demonstrating loyalty to your subordinates is the quickest way to get it in return. Most people want to believe in something and are very comfortable devoting themselves to something bigger than they are, say, the "cause" of the company. However, they do not want to be hoodwinked. They do not want to find themselves embarrassed because they devoted themselves on a one-way street. In simple terms, they will perform their job, and in their loyalty to you, they expect you will perform yours and be loyal to them. They expect you will cover their backs when required, and that is your job.

Two-way communication is another way to take care of your team. Certainly you have a mass of information to communicate to them, and they deserve to be kept informed as much as reasonably possible. Many, many managers believe keeping people in the dark is a means of protecting them from bad news or of maintaining a certain amount of power and control over them. This may be necessary if your employees are nine years old. Otherwise, keep them informed. They are adults, and they deserve to know the full truth. Likewise, offer open ears to their discussions. They are adults, and they deserve to be heard. It is now incumbent on you to have the fortitude to hear and truly listen to their ideas, positions, and concerns. Obviously, the larger your team, the harder this becomes, but you can still focus effectively on your smaller circles. At any rate, at any level, if they know you are listening, they will know you care about them and their opinions.

Along the line of loyalty, is the two-way street of respect. This must be shared. To expand on the earlier discussion of your respect for team members, you must not only surround yourself with people you respect, but you must let them know, and treat them with the respect they deserve. Once they have earned your respect, ensure they know you respect their opinions, their expertise, and their intellect. Similarly, work to earn their respect. Know your job; do your job; and, do it well. Earn their respect by living up to the highest standards. Do it by simply being trustworthy. It sounds so simple, yet viewing the evening news will show corporate America constantly finds itself in trouble because of a pure lack of trustworthiness.

The give and take impact of the responsibility and authority dynamic also warrants a close look. As you build and get to know your team, you will get familiar with how much authority to extend to any given member. You must learn to empower your team members with authority. You will determine how much authority based on intelligence, loyalty, trust, and confidence. On the other hand, you must bear the ultimate responsibility for your team. This takes fine craftsmanship, as well as significant courage. Knowing they are ultimately responsible, many managers keep control of all authority. This is not good team building. Get to know precisely where you can trust to extend the authority, and do it. The team and the team members will be better for it, and so will you. That is on the *give*, but on the *take*, be prepared to take full responsibility if something goes wrong. That is your job.

Finally, there is the two-way street of compassion. Good managers and leaders care, great ones have a genuine compassion for their subordinates. If it is clear you do not care about your organization or the people in it, your team members will not care either. However, if you have genuine compassion for your organization, what you are doing, and the people around you, the chances are better the people will care, too. When they care about their jobs, they will have a tendency to perform better. Granted, this is not open and shut, and not one hundred percent, but as you surround yourself with those great people, you owe it to them to show them your compassion. Those great people will in turn, bring their own personal compassion to their work.

IN CONCLUSION

If you have received anything out of this reading, the hope is you have recognized the fact that great management is not about you. It is all about the people who surround you. Ideally, you seek and select great people with all the right characteristics for all the right places at all the right times. If not, you cultivate what you have into the greatness you need. Then, most importantly, you do your utmost to take care of them, to show them how important they are to you. The box of tools that leads to successful management is enormous and packed tightly with a plethora of ideas, concepts, practices, and techniques that will help you become a great manager. A simple way to start is by surrounding yourself with great people and then taking care of them.

About Denise Williams:

Denise Williams spent thirty years in the United States Army proudly serving her country and the soldiers who worked for her. Before retiring as a Colonel, she held various command and staff positions. Her career highlight was commanding a brigade of 1500 electrical engineers and information technology specialists, while managing an annual budget of $300 million. She also spent time developing and instructing courses for senior military officers and government leaders on strategic leadership at the National Defense University in Washington, DC. While attending the Army War College, she authored a paper on Toxic Leadership that has been referenced and used for instruction across the Army. She is currently committed to passing on the knowledge gained from her experiences to young leaders. Her website is:

www.DistinctiveLeadershipDevelopment.com

and she can be reached at:

DFWilliams.Leadership@consultant.com

Notes

Notes

Notes

Notes

Notes

Notes